TERESA
OF AVILA

THE CROSSROAD SPIRITUAL LEGACY SERIES

Edited by John Farina

The Rule of Benedict: Insights for the Ages
  by Joan Chittister, O.S.B.

Ignatius Loyola: Spiritual Exercises
  by Joseph A. Tetlow, S.J.

Francis de Sales: Introduction to the Devout Life
and Treatise on the Love of God
  by Wendy M. Wright

St. Francis of Assisi: Writings for a Gospel Life
  by Regis J. Armstrong, O.F.M. Cap.

Teresa of Avila: Mystical Writings
  by Tessa Bielecki

Augustine: "God Is My Teacher" – Essential Writings
  by Benedict J. Groeschel

Thomas Aquinas: Spiritual Master
  by Robert Barron

TERESA
OF AVILA

MYSTICAL WRITINGS

Tessa Bielecki

CROSSROAD • NEW YORK

This printing: 1999

The Crossroad Publishing Company
370 Lexington Avenue, New York, NY 10017

Printed in the United States of America

Library of Congress Cataloging-in-Publication Data
Bielecki, Tessa.
    Teresa of Avila : mystical writings / Tessa Bielecki.
      p.   cm. — (The Crossroad spiritual legacy series)
    Includes bibliographical references.
    ISBN 0-8245-2504-3
    1. Teresa, of Avila, Saint, 1515–1582. 2. Mysticism—Catholic
Church—History—16th century. 3. Mysticism—Spain—History—16th
century. 4. Catholic Church—Doctrines—History—16th century.
I. Teresa, of Avila, Saint, 1515–1582. Selections. English.
1994. II. Title. III. Series.
BX4700.T4B52   1994
282′.092—dc20   94-7439
                                                   CIP

Grateful acknowledgment is hereby given for permission to use excerpts of
previously published material:

From *The Collected Works of St. Teresa of Avila* Volume One translated by Kieran
Kavanaugh and Otilio Rodriguez © 1976 by Washington Province of Discalced
Carmelites ICS Publications 2131 Lincoln Road, N.E. Washington, D.C. 20002
U.S.A.

From *The Collected Works of St. Teresa of Avila* Volume Two translated by Kieran
Kavanaugh and Otilio Rodriguez © 1980 by Washington Province of Discalced
Carmelites ICS Publications 2131 Lincoln Road, N.E. Washington, D.C. 20002
U.S.A.

From *The Collected Works of St. Teresa of Avila* Volume Three translated by Kieran
Kavanaugh and Otilio Rodriguez © 1985 by Washington Province of Discalced
Carmelites ICS Publications 2131 Lincoln Road, N.E. Washington, D.C. 20002
U.S.A.

From *The Letters of Saint Teresa of Jesus* Volumes One and Two translated by
Professor E. Allison Peers. Reprinted by permission of Burns & Oates Ltd.

For my mother and father,
who gave me the name Teresa at my christening,
and for my communities at Nada and Nova Nada,
who evoke the meaning of the name
through an ongoing christening.

Contents

Foreword

Writing in the fourth century a North African Christian by the name of Lactantius offered the following definition of virtue. For him, virtue is nothing less than "enduring of evils and labors." How unlike contemporary notions this definition of virtue is and how odd it sounds for us to be told so plainly that the fullness of life can be had only through enduring evils and trials. Yet, despite our inclination to write off Lactantius as an overly pessimistic nay-sayer, we must admit that life does include a large dose of suffering. We can take it well or badly. We can flee it or embrace it, but it will come and find us wherever we hide, and then it will test our mettle. Virtue does involve suffering evils, not simply actualizing ourselves, or conquering our fears, or visualizing success, or learning techniques to cope with stress, or building better "relationships" with members of the opposite sex. There are things in life that simply cannot be so easily manipulated. Situations that don't get better. Unpleasant realities that won't go away. Where do we turn when confronted by them?

We can turn to the externals, to our comforts and our conveniences, to the superficialities of our lives, or we can turn to our depths. Many who have lived before us have learned the hard way that turning to the depths is the way to a fuller life. Their insights have been handed down, often in forms that are now hard to find and harder to read. Their language is archaic. Their morality out of sync with ours. Their clarity, offputting. Their humility, disconcerting. Yet they are there, waiting quietly to share with us their hard-won wisdom, waiting to dialog with us as we face situations that are different from those they encountered only in the particulars, not in the essences.

Simply put, that is the reason why Crossroad, myself, and a team of well-known scholars and spiritual leaders have joined together to undertake the Spiritual Legacy series. The need for spiritual wisdom is great. Our situation is critical. This then is more than an enterprise in scholarship, more than a literary exercise. It is an effort to convey life.

Certainly the idea of doing editions of the works of spiritual guides from the past is not new. There are a host of books available that do just that. How is the Spiritual Legacy series different?

The uniqueness of this series abides in its content and its style. In content it endeavors to present both texts from the spiritual guide and extensive commentary by a present-day disciple of the sage. It gives the reader the chance to encounter for herself the writings of a spiritual master. Nothing can take the place of that experience. However demanding it might be, whatever efforts it might require, there can be no substitute for it. One, for instance, cannot simply hear a description of the tenth chapter of Augustine's *Confessions*. No commentary, however skilled, can take the place of reading for oneself Augustine's words of unparalleled power: "Late have I loved Thee, O Beauty, so ancient, yet so new!"

While it is true that there is no substitute for encountering the text firsthand, it is also certain that for most people that encounter will be an excursion into a foreign land. Often many centuries and numerous barriers of language, customs, philosophy, and style separate us from the writings of bygone sages. To come to that point where we can understand the horizon of the author, we must be taught something about the historical context, the literary style, and the thought forms of the age, for instance. That is why we have included in this series extensive commentary on the text. That commentary is alternated with the text throughout the books, so that one can be taught, then experience the writings firsthand, over and over as one moves deeper into the text. At that point, the horizon of the reader meets that of the author, aided by the expert guidance of the editor of each book, who suggests not only what the text might mean, but how it might be made part of our lives.

The style of the Spiritual Legacy series is also unique in that it attempts to convey life with a certain degree of sophistication that befits an educated readership. Yet it does not assume that everyone will have a background in the material presented, nor does it purport to offer original or arcane scholarship. The editors' mastery of the texts is in each case complemented by their experience in putting the meaning of the texts into practice and helping others to do so as well. We are trying to present a series of books that will fit somewhere between the scholarly editions that pride themselves on their accuracy and originality and the popular pieces that offer too little substance for the healthy reader.

The series is designed to be used by a broad range of people. For those seekers who wish to journey toward spiritual wholeness as part of a group, the series is ideally suited. The texts presented can be easily divided into sections for discussion by a group meeting, say, on a weekly basis.

For those who are traveling alone, the series is a trustworthy and enjoyable tour book. The direct, simple language of the commentaries frames the memorable words of the classical texts and offers them in an attractive setting for meditation and practical application.

The publisher and editors of the Spiritual Legacy series join me in inviting you to undertake a journey that will take you back to an encounter with ancient wisdom and challenge you to an experience of self-understanding and, at its best, self-transcendence. It is our hope that that experience will help you to grow and to be a source of fresh life for all those around you.

John Farina

Acknowledgments

I wrote this book in a rustic hogan (an eight-sided dwelling similar to that of the Navajos) a few miles from our Colorado monastery. The hogan, where I lived for eighteen weeks, had no running water or electricity, but vast silence, solitude, and vistas of the Sangre de Cristo Mountains and the San Luis Valley. San Isabel Creek runs nearby, with its towering cottonwoods: cold sentinels during the snowy weeks when I cross-country skied to and from my jeep, and comforting shade-makers when the summer sun baked the earth until it bloomed. When I began writing, I built a fire daily and watched ferocious winter snowstorms sweep across the valley that once was home to thousands of buffalo. Then, gradually, spring climbed up the slopes of the Sangres, left wildflowers in its wake, and sent torrents of snowmelt down the creek. Antelope bucks snorted and cow elk grazed with their calves as I wrote on into high summer, when the sun turned the green desert into a sea of rustling, dry seed heads. The austere topography was a mirror of St. Teresa's Castile, of her soul, and mine as well.

I am deeply grateful to Gary and Joanne Boyce, who let me live in their hogan. And to Father William McNamara, O.C.D., the most Teresian of contemporary Carmelites and my soul-friend, for his definitions of eros; mysticism; personal passionate presence; and the transparent and opaque personality.

With great joy I thank my community in Crestone, Colorado, who helped enormously with the research for this study and did all the typing — from my handwritten manuscript — and my community in Kemptville, Nova Scotia, who supported me lovingly from afar.

Special thanks to our friends in the Washington Province

of Discalced Carmelites who granted permission to quote from *The Collected Works of St. Teresa of Avila,* volumes 1–3, which were translated by Kieran Kavanaugh and Otilio Rodriguez. These translations are the best in English today and are available through ICS Publications, 2131 Lincoln Rd., N.E., Washington, D.C. 20002.

Mother Tessa Bielecki
October 15, 1993
Feast of St. Teresa of Avila
Crestone, Colorado

Abbreviations

F   *Foundations*

IC   *The Interior Castle*

L   *Life*

Le   *Letters*

P   *Poetry*

S   *Soliloquies*

SS   *Meditations on the Song of Songs*

T   *Spiritual Testimonies*

W   *The Way of Perfection*

Introduction

Let nothing disturb you,
Nothing dismay you.
All things are passing,
God never changes.
Patient endurance
Attains all things....
God alone suffices.

(Teresa's Bookmark)

Teresa of Avila was a towering personality who moved easily in and out of many worlds. She was a maddeningly beautiful young girl with an irrepressible zest for life; a passionate bride of Christ ardently longing to give herself totally to the Beloved; an affectionate mother of many men and women, who cooked well and recognized God in the kitchen. She was a shrewd businesswoman who knew how to negotiate a contract, drive a hard bargain, and fight her way through many a lawsuit; a rugged Zen master, leading us away from mental abstractions into a dynamic world grounded in experience; a wizened Indian grandmother with venerable knowledge of what ails and heals both body and soul.

Teresa's great sense of humor led to hilarious observations on the human condition. She had a tender penchant for sending gifts and composing verses and loved to write with exclamation points. She sang, danced, and played the tambourine to cheer her friends.

All this while living as a sixteenth-century Spanish nun who founded the Discalced Carmelites and inspired a school of spirituality that continues to enliven thousands of men and women today.

Teresa's story is not a quaint museum piece, charming but irrelevant. Her story is our story. We are called to immerse ourselves in the sempiternal Teresian spirit and live it out in the hurly-burly of our busy, technological, modern world.

Teresa was both a sensuous woman and a "strong man," as she put it, enjoying the fullness of man-womanhood. She had an irresistible combination of holiness and eros: a reaching and stretching of the whole body-person for the fullness of life.

Her writings are classic, contemporaneous with every age. Because they are primordial — concerned with fundamental human questions — they are also perennial: as relevant to our century as to those that preceded us and those that will follow.

This book presents the human Teresa as well as the canonized saint. We must not overspiritualize her, for she was diametrically opposed to "angelism" and insisted on taking the human component seriously. God does not transform us in a vacuum, but in the stuff of our everyday human existence. We live in a concrete context: a place and time, a cultural and spiritual milieu, peopled with family, friends, and sometimes enemies, with high aspirations and bitter disappointments.

We cannot simply study Teresa's writings. We must look at the way she lived. Abstract spiritual principles are only minimally helpful. Clothed in the flesh and blood circumstances of a particular human struggle, these principles take on power. Life, after all, is not an idea, but a drama.

The Life

Teresa was born on March 28, 1515, in Avila, "City of Knights," where even the churches looked like fortresses. Spain was constantly at war during her lifetime, and Avila, famous for its martial tradition, furnished captains and contingents for the battlefields of Italy, France, Germany, the Netherlands, North Africa, and the New World. The warrior spirit was stamped indelibly on Teresa's personality. Even when she described the spiritual life to her brother Lorenzo years later, she used martial imagery: "We ought to act as if we were at war — as, indeed, we are — and never relax until we have won the victory."

Teresa's father, Don Alonso de Cepeda, was the son of a Jewish merchant from Toledo. He was wealthy at the time of Teresa's birth, loving splendor and fine apparel. A devout Catholic, he lived with sword in one hand and rosary beads in the other. After his first wife died, leaving him a small son and daughter, he married Teresa's beautiful and intelligent mother, Beatriz de Ahumada, who was only fourteen. She died at the age of thirty-three, leaving the fourteen-year-old Teresa confused and bereaved.

Teresa had only two sisters. María was ten years older and as serious as her father. Juana was thirteen years younger. Seven of Teresa's nine brothers sailed with conquistadors to Peru, Argentina, Ecuador, Colombia, and Chile. Four of them were killed in the New World, and only Lorenzo and Pedro returned to Spain in Teresa's lifetime.

When Teresa entered adolescence, she realized she was naturally attractive and became vain, caught up in the desire to look pretty, fussing over her hair and hands, perfumes, and orange dresses with black velvet bands. This vanity reappeared throughout her life, still charmingly evident at age sixty-one. In 1575, one of her friars, a former Italian artist, painted her portrait, still preserved by the Seville convent. When Teresa saw it, she said, "May God forgive you, Fray Juan, for you have made me look like a bleary-eyed old hag!"

In her early teens, the motherless Teresa was befriended by a frivolous female cousin who distracted her from the piety of her youth. She was still enamored of the chivalric tales she'd hidden from her father and read with her mother as they threw dried lavender onto the glowing embers of the *brasero*, filling the room with sweet perfume and blue smoke. Teresa longed to be loved passionately, as the ladies in these romances were adored by their gallant and usually illicit lovers. She flirted, danced, and fell in love. With her maids and her cousin as accomplices, she smuggled love letters past her father, trembled over the replies, and arranged a secret rendezvous. Did this love turn into a full-blown affair? Most scholars say no, and Teresa left it ambiguous. But she did admit that her honor was at stake, and she endangered the lives of her father and brothers. The worried Don Alonso sent his vivacious daughter to the convent school of Our Lady of Grace in 1531.

Under the influence of the Augustinian nuns, Teresa recaptured the spiritual fervor of her childhood. But her fiery temperament was constrained by convent life, and the inner struggle she suffered over the pros and cons of becoming a nun seriously damaged her health. She recovered at home with her father, happily returned to her worldly life, yet remained haunted by the idea of a religious vocation. Not wanting to lose his favorite daughter, Don Alonso would not grant permission for her to join the convent.

"God loves courageous spirits," Teresa wrote. She herself had a lion's share of this virtue, which appeared early in her life. At age seven she ran away with her brother Rodrigo to the land of the Moors, hoping to be martyred for Christ. Now, in 1535, at age twenty, she defied her father once more and entered the Monastery of the Incarnation, despite the intense pain: "When I left my father's house I felt that separation so keenly that the feeling will not be greater, I think, when I die. For it seemed that every bone in my body was being sundered. Since there was no love of God to take away my love for my father and relatives, everything so constrained me that if the Lord hadn't helped me, my reflections would not have been enough for me to continue on. In this situation He gave me such courage against myself that I carried out the task."

It was not virtue that led Teresa to seek martyrdom at the hands of the Moors, but self-interest, since martyrs went straight to heaven. Nor was it virtue that led her to the Monastery of the Incarnation, but the fear of hell, the corollary of her earlier longing for heavenly bliss. Entering the convent was a joyless spiritual elopement. Teresa forced herself through sheer will power. In her initial struggles, the determined girl learned that God blesses "those who use force with themselves to serve Him," and in 1537, she professed her vows as a nun — and fell ill once again.

The crisis that precipitated her first illness revolved around whether or not to become a nun. The crisis that precipitated this second illness centered on the integrity of her vocation: How was she to live out her destiny as a professed religious woman? Teresa's father took her home again, but her health did not improve. So in 1538 he sent her to a *curandera* (folk healer) in Becedas. The cure of the *curandera* was worse than the illness. The herbal potions, vomitives, and purgatives — a kind of medieval shock therapy — almost killed Teresa. "The severity of the heart pains, which I went to have cured, was more acute," she wrote in her *Life*. "For sometimes it seemed that sharp teeth were biting into me."

Back in her father's house, she lapsed into a four-day coma and was pronounced dead. Her friends and family grieved, and the nuns at the Incarnation convent dug her grave. Teresa dramatically awakened, narrowly saved from the horror of being buried alive, but still found herself in great pain and now paralyzed. She moved back to the convent and spent the next three years as an invalid in the convent infirmary. "When I began to go about on hands and knees, I praised God," she movingly explained. In 1542, Teresa regained full use of her limbs and attributed her cure to St. Joseph, whom she lovingly called "this father and lord of mine."

Despite this stunning recovery, which was also a period of major spiritual growth, the next twelve years were a source of shame for Teresa. She lapsed back into her old habits and dispersed her energies. She had always been an extroverted, charming, and scintillating conversationalist. Now, back from the dead, Teresa was more vibrant and magnetic than ever. She once again frequented the convent parlor or *locutorio*, a sociable place where visitors from all walks of life came to talk about spiritual matters — interspersed with worldly news and even local gossip. Teresa soon became the parlor favorite, and naturally inclined as she was toward vanity, the attention went to her head. She was captivated by inordinate friendships with some of the guests and distracted by their frivolous conversations. She even went so far as to abandon prayer for over a year. She summarizes this double life poignantly: "Neither did I enjoy God nor did I find happiness in the world. When I was experiencing the enjoyments of the world, I felt sorrow when I recalled what I owed to God. When I was with God, my attachments to the world disturbed me. This is a war so troublesome that I don't know how I was able to suffer it even for a month, much less for many years." After "wasting" this period of her life in near mediocrity, during Lent of 1554, she experienced a radical conversion before a statue of Christ scourged at the pillar and never again regressed.

Teresa was now thirty-nine years old and had survived her midlife crisis. Leaving behind years of fragmentation, with her priorities ordered again, her mystical life began to grow. She became a true bride of Christ and received what is called the "grace of spiritual betrothal" in 1556. In 1560, after almost two years of visions of the risen Christ, she received the grace of "transverberation." In this wounding, Teresa felt a shining angel plunge a flaming golden arrow several times into her heart: "When he drew it out, I thought he was carrying off with him the deepest part of me; and he left me all on fire with great love of God." The marriage of convenience Teresa had forced upon herself by joining the convent now became the great passion of her life. Her longing for a chivalrous lover and all the romantic fantasies of her girlhood were fulfilled beyond her wildest imaginings.

But these powerful experiences often confused Teresa. She sought the counsel of her friends and Jesuit confessors. A few understood her, but most did not and tormented her further by suggesting that she was under the influence of diabolical powers. Though she was discreet, her experiences were the talk of Avila, causing her deeper humiliation. These years of misunderstanding were among her most tortured, and she describes them vividly in her *Life* in terms of the fear of insanity. Eventually assured by St. Peter of Alcántara that her spiritual favors were from God, Teresa began to live in peace. But not for long.

In 1560, at age forty-five, Teresa began to write the story of her life and to discuss her dream of a new monastic foundation with the friends and relatives who frequented her cell at the Monastery of the Incarnation. After two years of secret and often traumatic preparations, described below in the chapter entitled "Dare the Dream," the new Monastery of St. Joseph's was dedicated in Avila on August 24, 1562. Doña Teresa de Ahumada became the simple Discalced (shoeless) Teresa de Jesús. Her spiritual daughters began to call her "la Madre" (Mother). The next five years were quiet and happy ones for Teresa. She instructed her growing number of followers in her reformed way of life and wrote the constitutions for St. Joseph's, *The Way of Perfection*, and her ecstatic *Meditations on the Song of Songs*.

Then in 1567, her peace was disrupted again. A Franciscan missionary from Mexico visited St. Joseph's and upset Teresa with his stories of how many in the New World had never heard the name of Christ. Teresa's response was intense: "I was so grief-stricken over the loss of so many souls that I couldn't contain myself. I went to a hermitage with many tears. I cried out to the Lord, begging Him that He give me the means to be able to do something.... [O]ur Lord represented Himself to me in His usual way. He showed me much love, manifesting His desire to comfort me, and said: 'Wait a little, daughter, and you will see great things.' These words remained so fixed in my heart that I could not forget them. No matter how much I thought about this promise I couldn't figure out how it would be possible, nor was there a way of even imagining how it could come about."

In April, Juan Bautista Rubeo, father general of the Carmelite order, visited from Rome and authorized Teresa to found other monasteries. She had waited, as Christ had told her, and now she was about to see "great things." La Madre became "la Madre Fundadora" (Mother Foundress).

At age fifty-two, Teresa took to the road like a true knight errant, with a strenuous burden of work that would have taxed the strength of a youthful person in the peak of health. Untiringly she traveled in her squeaky, springless cart, on wretched roads, in all directions through the Spanish countryside. For the next eight years, la Madre Fundadora bartered and bargained, argued, arranged, and organized. In the midst of innumerable obstacles, ego conflicts, and absurdities, the aging and ailing woman preserved her smiling courage and the cheerful heart of a girl delighting in high adventure. She founded Medina del Campo in August 1567 and first met St. John of the Cross there. Malagón and Valladolid followed in 1568, Toledo and Pastrana in 1569. Salamanca was founded in 1570 and Alba de Tormes in 1571 with the help of St. John.

In October 1571, against her wishes, Teresa was installed as prioress back at the Monastery of the Incarnation, where she was not welcome. She invited John of the Cross to be chaplain there, and together they brought harmony and a high degree of spirituality to the rebellious convent. With St. John as her personal spiritual guide, Teresa received the grace of spiritual marriage in late 1572. She began writing her *Foundations* the following year.

Her term as prioress coming to an end, Teresa founded the Segovia monastery in March 1574, again with the help of St. John of the Cross. In April, after years of tyranny at the hands of their overbearing benefactress, the princess of Eboli, the Pastrana nuns escaped secretly to the Segovia monastery. (After the death of her illustrious husband, the princess had insisted on joining the convent, even though she was five months pregnant with her last child! She created havoc in the community, kept her servants, and demanded to be treated like a princess.) The vengeful princess then denounced Teresa's *Life* to the Inquisition.

For Teresa, 1575 was a pivotal year. In February she made the new foundation in Beas. In April she met Jerónimo Gracián, who became her confidant and best friend and changed the course of her life. Gracián's mother was the daughter of the Polish ambassador to Madrid. The bald and stocky Gracián was a complex character with both outstanding virtues and flaws. Teresa believed he was sent by God and the Blessed Mother to assist her in the increasingly exhausting work of her Carmelite Reform. In a letter to the king, she called Gracián "my helper" and wrote: "I had been suffering from these Fathers of the Cloth [the Calced Carmelites] for more than seventeen years, with not a soul to help me, and it was too much for my poor strength — I did not know how to bear it any longer." Now she hoped to "take a rest from governing these houses."

In May 1575, Gracián sent Teresa to found the monastery in Seville with María de San José as the first prioress. Teresa's brother Lorenzo returned from America in August with his young children — Lorenzo, Francisco, and Teresita. In December, Teresa was denounced to the Inquisition again, once more by a vengeful woman who had been expelled from the new Seville foundation. At the end of the year, the struggles between Teresa's Discalced Reform and the Calced Carmelites escalated. Rubeo, who originally told Teresa to make as many foundations as the hairs on her head, now turned against her because of false information. Teresa was ordered to return to one of her convents in Castile. The persecution of the Teresian Reform lasted three years, from 1576 until 1579. Teresa spent the first year in Toledo and the second two in Avila. During this time of terrible anxiety, when her life's work was in jeopardy, Teresa continued her *Foundations* and wrote her best synthesis, *The Interior Castle*. All her warrior energy was galvanized during this period: "I cannot help doing all that lies in my power, and using every means at my disposal, to prevent the ruin of these good beginnings of ours," she wrote to her Portuguese friend, Don Teutonio de Braganza. Teresa struggled with even greater determination from her "imprisonment" and fought "like a desperado." She was desperate indeed, but despite her occasional fits of fear and worry, she kept a light heart and joked with Lorenzo: "These affairs of ours do teach us what the world is like: really, it is as good as a play!"

When the persecutions ended, Teresa began traveling again at age sixty-four. She fell seriously ill during the influenza epidemic of 1580 and almost died. Until then, Teresa carried her six decades with the grace of youth. Now she was suddenly an old woman. "I'm nothing but a poor old hag," she said. Her head twitched with a nervous trembling, and she could not move without a cane. Increasingly frequent heart attacks kept her periodically confined to bed. She now wore glasses and still could not use her broken left arm or dress herself. "For the love of God," she wrote Gracián earlier, "be careful not to have any falls on those roads, for since I have had my arm in this state, I have grown more worried about that. It is still swollen, and so is the hand, and I have a saffron plaster on which is like a coat of mail."

Despite her infirmities, Teresa made new foundations in Villanueva de la Jara and Palencia in 1580. "As I am still living," she wrote María de San José, "I must tell you how I long to do something for God's service: I cannot live much longer and I would not spend the remaining years as idly as I have spent those just past: all I have done is to suffer interiorly — there is nothing else whatever to show for them. Pray God, all of you, to give me strength to spend myself a little in His service." Nothing whatever to show for the past years? The Discalced Reform was well on the way toward a legal separation from the Calced Carmelites, which became official through a papal brief on June 22, 1580. In 1581, a pivotal meeting in Alcalá confirmed new constitutions, and Gracián became the first provincial, to Teresa's utter joy.

That summer, she made the foundation in Soria. After New Year's 1582, she left Avila for the last time to begin the foundation in Burgos while John of the Cross made the foundation in Granada with Ana de Jesús. Burgos was one of the most difficult foundations, and Teresa tells the story in detail with exquisite patience. The shaky handwriting in her original manuscript shows her increasing exhaustion and deterioration.

The last years of Teresa's life were beset with many disillusionments. María Bautista, though close to her as both relative and friend, became too independent. The leader in Salamanca, another relative, created scandal trying to purchase an expensive house. The reputation of Teresa's niece, Beatriz, was damaged by rumors of an adulterous affair with a friend of her parents, who remained inert. "Do something or other, for the love of God, or you will be the death of me," she wrote the girl's father. Her nephew's in-laws were threatening a lawsuit over Lorenzo's will, and Teresa was executrix. The nuns in Alba de Tormes were in trouble with their major patroness. Ana de Jesús disobeyed Teresa's orders over the foundation in Granada. Antonio de Heredia was jealous of Gracián and bickering pettily. Her brother Pedro was severely depressed, and Teresa was "dreadfully apprehensive of some disaster." Worst of all, Gracián seemed to abandon her when she most missed and needed him. She suffered these trials heroically, by practicing what she preached: "Fix your eyes on the Crucified and everything will become small for you."

The story of Teresa's final journey, sickness, and death is heartrending. After a tortuous trip ordered by the vindictive Antonio, Teresa reached Alba de Tormes on September 20, 1582, at 6 P.M., completely exhausted. "It's been twenty years since I went to bed so early," she said. On September 29, she announced her imminent death and never got up again. On October 3, she received the Sacrament of Extreme Unction and made her last confession. She urged the nuns around her to be faithful to the rule and the constitutions. "Do not imitate the poor example set you by this bad nun," she said humbly, "but forgive me." When the Blessed Sacrament was brought into the room, Teresa struggled to her knees and wanted to prostrate herself. "My Lord and my Bridegroom!" she cried out. "The longed-for hour has come! Now is the time for us to meet, my Lord and my Beloved!" After receiving Communion, Teresa repeated over and over again: "I am a daughter of the Church!"

The last night was one of great pain as Teresa slowly bled to death from what modern doctors now think was cancer of the uterus. She prayed the church's finest penitential psalm over and over: "My sacrifice, O God, is a contrite spirit; a heart contrite and humbled, O God, you will not spurn." The next evening, October 4, the feast of St. Francis of Assisi, Teresa of Avila died at age sixty-seven in the arms of Ana de San Bartholomé. Since the new Gregorian calendar was introduced that year, the day following Teresa's death became October 15, still celebrated as her feast day.

Only thirty-two years after her death, Teresa was beatified by Pope Paul V in 1614. On March 12, 1622, she was canonized by Pope Gregory XV. On September 27, 1970, Pope Paul VI declared Teresa the first woman doctor of the church.

The Writings

Teresa wrote over one thousand pages of reflections, prayers, and poetry. Her 450 extant letters comprise another one thousand pages. Instead of treating each of the works separately, this book focuses on the entire Teresian corpus as a whole and proceeds according to the overarching themes that Teresa weaves through all her works. Teresa's conversational writing style is both aggravating and captivating. She often criticizes herself for saying too much and seems to understand that we have to wade through a mountain of verbiage to get to the heart of the matter.

But Teresa's writing is happily like her personality: lavish, extravagant, and even flamboyant. She writes the way she lived — with zest and enthusiasm. She spontaneously and repeatedly cries out, "Oh!" from the depths of her being. In her *Soliloquies* alone, which comprises only twenty pages, she uses "Oh!" more than ninety-three times — sometimes three in a row!

She writes with freedom and spontaneity, revealing her inner depths easily but with discretion. *The Interior Castle* is a more serious theological treatise on the mystical life and, depending on one's point of view, is therefore either more or less appealing. Her *Life* is a conversation with her confessor and friend, García de Toledo. In *The Way of Perfection,* Teresa discusses fundamental requirements for the spiritual life and dialogues with her sisters, whom she also addresses as daughters and friends, illustrating her great capacity to relate to others in a variety of roles.

As though she were with us face-to-face, she addresses us as well and is uninhibited about her personal asides. Going off the subject time and again, she always catches herself ("Where was I? Oh, yes,...") and returns to her major theme. This is both maddening and delightful because her digressions are often her most passionate and important paragraphs. "So many things come to my mind," she tells us. "I wish I had many hands to write them all down at the same time, so I wouldn't forget anything!"

Because she speaks to us so intimately and often gets carried away, Teresa's writing is not always systematic. She calls it "rough" and "heavy," "jumbled" and "disordered." She shifts back and forth from first person to third, from past to present tense, and uses multiple verbs and superlatives. No one passage can be called her definitive statement on any topic because she may give a more nuanced or even contradictory opinion elsewhere.

Teresa wrote her major works out of obedience to confessors and spiritual directors. She claims she's like a parrot, who can do nothing but repeat. Yet she is original, and each one of her works has a deep interior order, despite the trying circumstances under which she wrote. She seldom had the luxury of time set aside expressly for writing and had to "steal" time here and there from her many vexing occupations — household chores, vast correspondence, spiritual counseling, administrative duties, and extensive travel. She never took time to read over what she wrote. She frequently wrote late into the night instead of sleeping, sitting on a cork mat on the floor of her room, using a quill pen and a stone bench for a desk. She was often interrupted for months at a time by illness or crisis.

How should one approach reading Teresa? Begin with her *Life*. Though not strictly an autobiography because it focuses more on her inner life, it does communicate enough concrete details of her first fifty years to help us see the similarity to our own lives.

Next turn to the *Spiritual Testimonies* and read number 58. Written for the Inquisition in Seville ten years after the *Life*, this testimony gives a six-page summary of what it will take Teresa over three hundred pages to flesh out in the *Life*. Testimony 59 presents her mystical terminology and a succinct picture of the state of her soul at this time. Testimony 65, written for her dear friend Dr. Alonso Velázquez in 1581, shows how Teresa grew from her early upheavals into extraordinary peace of soul. The *Soliloquies* offer concrete examples of Teresa's prayer.

Teresa's letters are perhaps her richest legacy because she wrote them with no inhibitions. They show us aspects of her personality not found in her other writings. As we read these letters, time stops, and we hear Teresa's voice as though she were standing right beside us — laughing, weeping, scolding, or teasing.

Teresa's *Foundations* describe the origins of each of the convents she founded. We must not dismiss this book as irrelevant, for it is full of ramifications for making our own personal dream come true. The pages of the *Foundations* also contain many universal spiritual counsels. But above all, they tell a gripping tale full of exciting adventures, freakish mishaps, and fascinating characters such as the beautiful, trouble-making, one-eyed princess of Eboli; the irresistible and charming Jerónimo Gracián; Beatriz Chaves, a dramatic example of sixteenth-century child abuse; Antonio de Heredia, Teresa's first friar; and Ambrosio Mariano, another early friar who was an engineer, a knight of the Order of St. John of Jerusalem, and chamberlain to the queen of Poland.

Another fascinating character who weaves in and out of Teresa's life is the devil himself. What are we to make of all this devil-talk? In our own day we are far more inclined to speak of our own internal demons than of the devil as a circumscribed entity "out there." On the one hand, this is healthy because it makes us assume responsibility for the evil we commit and create, instead of excusing ourselves by saying, "The devil made me do it!" On the other hand, it is naive, irresponsible, and dangerous to refuse to admit the existence of evil as a potent force outside ourselves, with a power beyond our own control, held at bay and indeed overcome only by the power of God, the All-Merciful One, working through our own feeble human instrumentality. Teresa's approach is actually quite contemporary and sophisticated: The devil is real; he acts in the world with powerful visibility, but the power of God is far greater.

Teresa was often embarrassed to write and found the task

difficult because of the ineffable nature of the mystical experience she tried to describe. She humbly speaks of her struggle and confusion, knowing that it is one thing to experience God, another to understand the experience, and yet another to know how to explain it. To help us, Teresa uses metaphors, comparisons, and vivid images drawn from every aspect of human life — nature, marriage, travel, economics, medicine, the kitchen, and the garden. She often wrote after receiving Communion, experiencing on the spot what she was writing about, while "His Majesty" (her favorite name for Christ) and the Holy Spirit moved her pen.

The Interior Castle is Teresa's masterpiece, written twelve years after the *Life*, when she was sixty-two. Honed and purified by vast experience of the human adventure, both temporal and spiritual, Teresa is clearly integrated and holy, a sage, and a saint. Many experts recommend that if we are to read only one of her works, it should be *The Interior Castle*, and that work does indeed synthesize her finest teaching. But if we begin and end there, we rob ourselves of all the pain and beauty Teresa suffered en route to the highest stage of spiritual development, which she calls the "Seventh Mansion." In the *Life* we find detailed evidence of the excruciating refining process we must undergo to find our lives at last distilled into a rare liqueur — exquisitely delicious and divinely intoxicating.

The Road Map

Teresa of Avila in sixteenth-century Spain grappled with the same basic issues we do as we move toward the twenty-first century: love and intimacy, friendships and family systems, dreams and devilish nightmares, suffering, woundedness, warring and wedding, bleeding and bedding, prayer and the mystery of God. Teresa outlines the spiritual dimension underlying every aspect of our lives: How do we set out on the spiritual journey? Or rather: How do we wake up and realize we are already on the royal road? What obstacles do we encounter? How do we overcome them? This book, in attempting to answer some of these questions, deals with Teresa's most crucial insights:

1. Life is both an earthy and a spiritual adventure, which Teresa calls the "royal road." We are not only bodies in an earthly exile but embodied souls with an eternal destiny — a destiny difficult to fulfill if we fall prey to selfishness and ego inflation.

2. Life is relatedness. Love and friendship are primary ingredients. But what do we mean by love? Real friendship is not only light, joy, and consolation but hard work, critical challenge, and anxious concern.

3. Life sparkles with the incomparable richness of the man-woman dynamic. In our painful era of male-bashing and the exploitation of women, Teresa helps us see the angelic and demonic dimensions of both the masculine and the feminine. Her own struggles with emotional addiction help men and women toward a more complementary partnership of interdependence and mutual admiration.

4. Life is nothing without a dream. How do we make our dream come true? Teresa shows us the courage and daring we need to leave the comfort zone and the warrior energy required to keep our dream alive.

5. Suffering is a mysterious and inescapable part of life — recognized or repressed, embraced or resisted. Grappling creatively with suffering, especially physical and emotional pain, is what we mean by "embracing the cross." For the Christian, suffering is not meaningless but redemptive. "The pay begins now!"

6. Life is prayer — not the empty recitation of words, but personal passionate presence. Teresa teaches us a form of meditation sorely needed in our day, offers good advice on focusing the wandering mind, and marvels over the Real Presence of the whole Christ in our world.

7. Our life of prayer is meant to be ecstatic intimacy with God, spiritual matrimony, and "holy madness." But we must distinguish genuine ecstasy from false absorption.

8. In our prayer we may sometimes experience secondary

psychophysical phenomena such as visions, locutions, and raptures. Some people call these "spiritual favors," and others call them the "spooky stuff." What are we to make of them? How do we distinguish between authentic and inauthentic spiritual experience?

9. As we move into deeper dimensions of life and love, we recognize signs of growth. How can we tell we are growing and not regressing? We experience spaciousness, spontaneity, emotional stability, deep peace, heroic service, and a powerful release of transforming energy, particularly through a mysterious reconciliation of opposites: triumph in struggle, rest in laboring, and serenity in sorrow.

The texts from Teresa's writings were carefully chosen because of their contemporary relevance. Though we may not always express ourselves the way Teresa did, we still ask the same basic questions and feel the same feelings.

Teresa imparts her spiritual legacy through more than principles and practices. Sometimes her personal example, a gesture, or a story teaches us more than all the maxims in the world. When we hear how this woman responded to the betrayal of a friend, a scandalous family problem, a financial crisis, bad health, depression, or loneliness, we are likely to be more inspired than we would be reading a mere principle or piece of advice removed from the concrete context from which it emerged.

The spiritual life is not an abstract, rarified affair relegated to periods of meditation and prayer, rituals and ceremonies, spiritual reading and guidance, our service and acts of charity. The spiritual life is our whole life. Above all, then, Teresa challenges us to live in the spirit of her beloved Jesus, who said: "I have come that you may have life and have it to the full" (John 10:10).

Chapter 1

The Royal Road

Do not stop on the road but, like the strong, fight even to death in the search, for you are not here for any other reason than to fight. You must always proceed with this determination to die rather than fail to reach the end of the journey.

(W 20.2)

Teresa took the body seriously, but she knew it was temporal, and her hunger was for the eternal. She teaches us not to limit ourselves to the body but to consider the far richer world of the soul. We must not imagine that we are hollow inside: "Within us lies something incomparably more precious than what we see outside ourselves." As Teresa wrote to Lorenzo: "As I go about to so many places, and so many people talk to me, I often don't know what to say, except that we are worse than beasts, since we fail to realize our souls' great dignity." We commit spiritual suicide — "soul-murder" — when we do not take the time to nurture the life of the soul and preserve its beauty, largely through prayer.

Teresa gives us exquisite descriptions of the human soul as a fresh and fecund tree, planted in living waters; a pearl from the Orient; a brightly polished mirror; or water in a glass. And in the center is Christ, our Lord. We do not have to go looking here and there outside to find him. He is not separate from us and far away but deep within ourselves in "this little heaven of our soul." Because Christ is so very near, we do not need to sprout wings and fly to heaven to find him or to shout at him to be heard.

This understanding is crucial for Teresa's method of meditation or recollection and forms the basis for *The Interior Castle*. She describes the soul as a castle made of clear crystal, magnificently spacious, with no less than a million dwelling places, traditionally called "mansions." We must not visualize the castle in a limited, linear way, room after room in neatly structured sequence. Since the King resides in the innermost dwelling place, the center is infinite, and therefore the inside is larger than the outside. Teresa uses the image of the palmetto, an edible Andalusian plant like the palm tree. But since only the tender heart of the palmetto is eaten, this image for the dwelling places does not seem accurate. We must understand that the most interior place, the Seventh Mansion, is both the largest and yet the center. As we continue to go in, each dwelling is larger than the last. In this rich castle image, Teresa conveys the incomparable beauty God has bestowed on us by dwelling within the human soul.

Beginning with Determination

Life, then, is not only an earthy adventure but a spiritual adventure. We call it the journey, the path, the quest. In the spirit of chivalry, Teresa called it the "royal road." "Do not be frightened," she said, "by the many things you need to consider in order to begin this divine journey which is the royal road to heaven. A great treasure is gained by traveling this road; no wonder we have to pay what seems to us a high price. The time will come when you will understand how trifling everything is next to so precious a reward."

Teresa is an outstanding spiritual guide along the royal road — practical, concrete, and down-to-earth. She emphasizes the importance of a good beginning. We must start with determination — a central theme that she repeats frequently. Since we act the way we think, in the beginning we must boldly and daringly cultivate high aspirations, and not settle for less: "For many remain at the foot of the mount who could ascend to the top."

Beginning well requires effort. This may mean initial difficulty and resistance, but these are soon swallowed up in our enthusiasm. We must lay a solid foundation and cultivate good habits of prayer, reading, and the practice of virtue. We must be humble enough to pay attention to little things. If we are careless in what seems insignificant, we open the door to bigger mistakes. If we neglect our spiritual reading one day because of fatigue, we may indulge ourselves and neglect it a second day. By the third day, our resolve seriously weakens, and we lose the habit altogether. Teresa considered reading sustenance for the soul — as necessary as food for the body. She loved to read good books and called them her recreation as well as her salvation. For over fifteen years she could not practice meditation without reading because of her overly active mind. She recommends the same discipline for those with a similar temperament.

Teresa is vehement about persevering all the way to the end of the royal road. She warns us against gradual backsliding. We need courage not to turn back and vigilance, for as long as we live, we will never have complete security. The road is fraught with many dangers, so we must be awake and alert. We must not stop in the middle or give up when inevitable difficulties come, but begin over and over again.

Our initial determination helps us progress. But then we make a few mistakes, encounter obstacles and roadblocks — and we falter. Rather ominously, but with humor and compassion, Teresa warns us: "If there is going to be a downfall, it's better that it happen in the beginning rather than later." Then she reminds us that God's love for us is so great that he can't bear to lose us and hence gives us "a thousand interior warnings" against a thousand pitfalls along the path.

Faltering and falling along the royal road is inevitable — and valuable. Sooner or later, our "cracks and imperfections" surface again, and we find our old vanities and weaknesses reawakening. Teresa urges us not to be discouraged because "there will always be failure as long as we live in this mortal body." We must trust in the healing mercy of God, who can draw good out of every failure and fall.

Teresa was not only a spiritual guide. She was also an astute psychologist long before the advent of contemporary psychology. She knew that self-knowledge is fundamental to human integration, while the lack of it leads to neurosis and psychosis. The spiritual practice of self-knowledge is crucial at every stage along the royal road, no matter how much we advance. It is sometimes even more valuable than prayer itself.

The Danger of Selfism

Teresa's incisive analysis of human nature led her to the same conclusions spiritual leaders from all traditions have made throughout the ages. What is the greatest obstacle to growth along the royal road? There are many names for it: the grasping, craving ego; selfishness; the vanity of self-esteem. Teresa used herself as a prime example, colorfully calling herself "filthy mud," "a rotten worm," and "foul-smelling."

What are we to make of her vision of humanity as a "malodorous dungheap"? Is Teresa excessively morbid, guilty, and negative? Does she exaggerate? Does she hate herself and humanity? No! If we were not so blinded by the self-absorption and self-aggrandizement of our narcissistic society, we would recognize the "selfism" that thwarts spiritual growth. The self-love, self-will, self-interest, and self-consciousness inherent in human nature destroy us if not acknowledged and curtailed through spiritual practice.

Through self-love, we make ourselves the center of the universe. Self-will makes us want our own way. Self-interest leads us to make decisions and manipulate people and situations to our own advantage, no matter how badly they affect others. When we are self-conscious, we are so full of self, we cannot allow anyone else a significant place in our vision of reality. We are our own worst enemies. If we cannot eradicate selfism, we become insufferable egotists, wreaking havoc within ourselves and in the world around us — in our marriages, families, and our short-sighted business practices around the globe.

"Among my faults I had this one...." " "I didn't like to suffer scorn...." " "I was extreme in my vain desire for my reputation." With these humble admissions, Teresa confesses her own struggles with selfism, her own preoccupation with "looking good," self-esteem, upward mobility, or what her era called "honor." Of course we need a healthy sense of self-worth, personal dignity, and a noble destiny. But obsession with status, prestige, or position makes Teresa's blood freeze. "Get rid of this pestilence," she commands us: "Cut off the branches as best you can, and if this is not enough, pull up the roots."

The vanity of self-esteem makes us look in the wrong places for personal worth — outside instead of inside, at material goods instead of inner value. We get caught up in the world's mendacity, the Big Lie, and falsely esteem money, possessions, social or economic status, rank, seniority, the prestige of some office. "But, oh, my Lord and my God, how the whole world's habit of getting involved in vanities vitiates everything!" If we do not watch ourselves, these concerns will poison us, for they "amount to nothing much more than a debate about whether the mud is better for making bricks or adobes!"

Today's world is tremendously preoccupied with questions of "rights." Though this is essential in the political arena, without a balanced perspective, it can be destructive on the spiritual level, spoiling families, communities, schools, offices, and man-woman relationships. It leads to inordinate preoccupation with "points of honor," protocol, and going through the "right channels," with distracting questions of whether or not we were offended, slighted, hurt, or insulted, with "I was right" and "You were wrong." Teresa doesn't know whether to laugh or cry over this absurdity. She tells us not to pay attention to these so-called wrongs, injuries, or offenses because they are really "nothings." Jesus taught us to forgive those who trespass against us because he knows we are so fond of our miserable "rights" that it's difficult for us to be forgiving.

Teresa had the opportunity to live for months at a time in the homes of wealthy patrons. Immersed in their own milieu, observing the time and energy they expended to "keep up appearances," she came to strong conclusions about the vanity and slavery of riches and high position. "This is a kind of subservience that makes calling such persons 'lords' one of the world's lies, for it doesn't seem to me that they are anything but slaves to a thousand things" — including rank and social obligations. When we read her criticisms of the outward trappings of a sixteenth-century king and his court minions, who would not be recognized without their showy displays of power, prestige, and importance, we are led to think of twentieth-century politicians, academicians, churchmen, bureaucrats, and executives with their own "guards" and titles of address, their protocol and people in waiting: "They have to have designated times for speaking and designated persons to whom they speak. If some poor little creature has any business matter to take up, what roundabout ways he must go through." In contrast, Teresa speaks ravishingly about the true majesty and *accessibility* of Christ, the King of kings.

The vanity of self-esteem leads us into another trap, and we become the slaves of public opinion: role-playing, people-pleasing, and following the crowd in order to gain approval. We are so afraid of what others may think and say about us that we become self-conscious instead of self-oblivious. We are so ready to do whatever "they" want of us that we end up compromising our integrity and offending God. What difference does it make what others think? We must stand our own ground despite public opinion and guard against having our heads turned when people praise us, for "never does the world exalt without putting down." Teresa was vehemently convinced that the search for human approval is futile: "Today people will think one thing, tomorrow another; at one time they will speak well of something; soon they will speak badly of it. May you be blessed, my Lord and my God, for You are unchangeable forever and ever, amen."

The vanity of self-esteem and preoccupation with human approval lead us to become soft and self-indulgent instead of challenging ourselves and stretching our limits. We seek rest instead of struggle, false security instead of holy insecurity, vapid peace instead of spiritual warfare. We become bourgeois, lax, lukewarm, and merely "ok" and "pretty good" — far from the heroism Teresa embodied in imitation of Jesus.

The surest antidotes to this mediocrity are searching self-knowledge, vigilance, and humility. Closely allied to these is obedience — a pivotal virtue the modern mind arrogantly finds difficult. All this spiritual practice is far more beneficial if we are assisted by a spiritual guide or "soul-friend." But it isn't always easy to find good spiritual direction. Teresa went for twenty years without finding anyone who understood her. She assures us that God will not abandon us, however, even if we cannot find a human director.

Whether we are married or single, monastic or lay, educated or not, all of us need soul-friending. Spending as much time as she did living with laypeople — merchants and nobles, soldiers and seamstresses, princes and paupers — Teresa speaks accurately about the spiritual dangers of selfism in those who live in their own homes without submitting to spiritual guidance.

In addition to "official" spiritual guidance, we can benefit enormously from soul-friending among our peers. "Disillusion me with truth," Teresa begged García de Toledo. With him and three other friends, Teresa made a "pact" to meet regularly together and in love and friendship to free one another from illusion. Ahead of her time in this as in so many other ways, Teresa organized a sixteenth-century "support group" and even a kind of "sensitivity session." She called the group together in secret, she explained, because "this kind of talk is no longer in fashion." Is the truth any more in fashion today?

Meditation

In the following texts Teresa eloquently describes the interior life of the soul as a castle made of diamond where the King of kings dwells. She encourages us in our journey along the royal road and emphasizes the value of determination and the way of the cross. She gives concrete examples of selfism and our miserable preoccupation with wealth, rights, praise, and points of honor. Teresa concludes with a call to obedience, humility, and spiritual guidance, especially for people who live as householders. Then we read the invitation she extended to friends to make a "pact of truth."

Teresian Texts: The Royal Road

It is a shame and unfortunate that through our own fault we don't understand ourselves or know who we are. Wouldn't it show great ignorance, my daughters, if someone when asked who he was didn't know, and didn't know his father or mother or from what country he came? Well now, if this would be so extremely stupid, we are incomparably more so when we do not strive to know who we are, but limit ourselves to considering only roughly these bodies. Because we have heard and because faith tells us so, we know we have souls. But we seldom consider the precious things that can be found in this soul, or who dwells within it, or its high value. Consequently, little effort is made to preserve its beauty. All our attention is taken up . . . with these bodies of ours.

(*IC* 1.1.2)

> And should by chance you do not know
> Where to find Me,
> Do not go here and there;
> But if you wish to find Me,
> *In yourself seek Me.*
>
> Soul, since you are My room,
> My house and dwelling,
> If at any time,
> Through your distracted ways
> I find the door tightly closed,
>
> Outside of yourself seek Me not,
> To find Me it will be
> Enough only to call Me,

Then quickly will I come,
And in yourself seek Me.

(*P* 8)

The soul is like a castle made entirely out of a diamond or a very clear crystal, in which there are many rooms, just as in heaven there are many dwelling places.... [T]he soul of the just person is nothing else but a paradise where the Lord says He finds His delight. So then, what do you think that the abode will be like where a King so powerful, so wise, so pure, so full of all good things takes His delight? I don't find anything comparable to the magnificent beauty of a soul and its marvelous capacity.

(*IC* 1.1.1)

You mustn't think of these dwelling places in such a way that each one would follow in file after the other; but turn your eyes towards the center, which is the room or royal chamber where the King stays, and think of how a palmetto has many leaves surrounding and covering the tasty part that can be eaten. So here, surrounding this center room are many other rooms; and the same holds true for those above. The things of the soul must always be considered as plentiful, spacious, large; to do so is not an exaggeration. The soul is capable of much more than we can imagine, and the sun that is in this royal chamber shines in all parts. It is very important for any soul that practices prayer, whether little or much, not to hold itself back and stay in one corner. Let it walk through these dwelling places which are above, down below, and to the sides, since God has given it such dignity.

(*IC* 1.2.8)

Wherever God is there is heaven.... Where His Majesty is present, all glory is present.... [T]here is no need to go to heaven in order to speak with one's Eternal Father or find delight in Him. Nor is there any need to shout. However softly we speak, He is near enough to hear us. Neither is there any need for wings to go to find Him. All one need do is go into solitude and look at Him within oneself, and not turn away from so good a Guest but with great humility speak to Him as to a father.

(W 28.2)

I consider it impossible for us to pay so much attention to worldly things if we take the care to remember we have a Guest such as this within us, for we then see how lowly these things are next to what we possess within ourselves.... You will laugh at me, perhaps, and say that what I'm explaining is very clear, and you'll be right; for me, though, it was obscure for some time. I understood well that I had a soul. But what this soul deserved and who dwelt within it I did not understand because I had covered my eyes with the vanities of the world.... If I had understood as I do now that in this little palace of my soul dwelt so great a King, I would not have left Him alone so often. I would have remained with Him at times and striven more so as not to be so unclean. But what a marvelous thing, that He who would fill a thousand worlds and many more with His grandeur would enclose Himself in something so small!...Since He is Lord He is free to do what He wants, and since He loves us He adapts Himself to our size.

(W 28.10–11)

❖

Don't pay any attention to the fears they raise or to the picture of the dangers they paint for you. Wouldn't it be nice if while desiring to procure a great treasure I should want to walk without danger along a path where there are so many robbers. It would be a pleasant world if they would let you get the treasure in peace. But for a penny's worth of self-interest they will go many nights without sleep and disturb you in body and soul. For when you are about to gain the treasure — or steal it, since the Lord says that the violent take it away — by a royal road and by a safe road, the road chosen by our King and all His elect and saints, they will tell you that there are so many dangers and so many things to fear. How many more dangers are there

for those who think they obtain this good without following a
road?

(W 21.5)

How they are to begin is very important — in fact, all important. They must have a great and very resolute determination
to persevere until reaching the end, come what may, happen
what may, whatever work is involved, whatever criticism arises,
whether they arrive or whether they die on the road, or even
if they don't have courage for the trials that are met, or if the
whole world collapses. You will hear some persons frequently
making objections: "there are dangers"; "so-and-so went astray
by such means"; "this other one was deceived"; "another who
prayed a great deal fell away"; "it's harmful to virtue"; "it's not
for women, for they will be susceptible to illusions"; "it's better
they stick to their sewing."

(W 21.2)

Have great confidence, for it is necessary not to hold back one's
desires, but to believe in God that if we try we shall little by little, even though it may not be soon, reach the state the saints
did with His help. For if they had never determined to desire
and seek this state little by little in practice they would never
have mounted so high. His Majesty wants this determination,
and He is a friend of courageous souls if they walk in humility
and without trusting in self. I have not seen any cowardly soul
or any of these who under the pretext of humility remain along
the bottom of this path who do not take many years to advance
as far as these courageous ones do in a few. I marvel at how important it is to be courageous in striving for great things along
this path.

(L 13.2)

It is an important matter for beginners in prayer to start off by
becoming detached from every kind of satisfaction and to enter the path solely with the determination to help Christ carry
the cross like good cavaliers, who desire to serve their king

at no salary since their salary is certain. We should fix our eyes on the true and everlasting kingdom which we are trying to gain.... Begin with the determination to follow the way of the cross and not desire consolations, since the Lord Himself pointed out this way of perfection saying: *take up your cross and follow me.* He is our model; whoever follows His counsels solely for the sake of pleasing Him has nothing to fear.

(L 15.11, 13)

The greatest labor is in the beginning because it is the beginner who works while the Lord gives the increase. In the other degrees of prayer the greatest thing is enjoying; although whether in the beginning, the middle, or the end, all bear their crosses even though these crosses be different. For all who follow Christ, if they don't want to get lost, must walk along this path that He trod. And blessed be the trials that even here in this life are so superabundantly repaid.

(L 11.5)

❖

If we tell a rich person living in luxury that it is God's will that he be careful and use moderation at table so that others might at least have bread to eat, for they are dying of hunger, he will bring up a thousand reasons for not understanding this save in accordance with his own selfish purposes. If we tell a backbiter that it is God's will that he love his neighbor as himself, he will become impatient and no reason will suffice to make him understand. We can tell a religious who has grown accustomed to freedom and comfort that he should remember his obligation to give good example and keep in mind that when he says these words they be not just words but be put into practice.... But it is just useless to insist nowadays with some of them.

(W 33.1)

What is it we buy with this money we desire? Is it something valuable? Is it something lasting? Oh, why do we desire it? Miserable is the rest achieved that costs so dearly. Frequently one obtains hell with money and buys everlasting fire and pain without end. Oh, if everyone would consider it unprofitable dirt, how many lawsuits would be avoided! What friendship there would be among all if there were no self-interest about honor and money!

(L 20.27)

When they tell us who their father was and about the millions they get in rent and of their title of dignity, there's no more to know. In fact, here below people in paying honor don't take into account the persons themselves, however much these persons may deserve the honor, but their wealth.... O miserable world!... where men pay attention not to what they have within themselves but to what their tenant farmers and vassals have.... It's something amusing to relax over when you all have to take some recreation. For this is a good pastime: to notice how blindly those who are in the world spend their time.

(W 22.4–5)

However small the point of honor may be, the concern for it is like that of sound coming from an organ when the timing or measure is off; all the music becomes dissonant. This concern is something that does damage to the soul in all areas, but in this path of prayer it is a pestilence.

(L 31.21)

If there is any vain esteem of honor or wealth (and this can be had inside monasteries as well as outside, although inside the occasions for it are more removed and the fault would be greater), you will never grow very much or come to enjoy the true fruit of prayer.

(W 12.5)

God, by His Passion, deliver us from dwelling on such words or thoughts as, "I have seniority," "I am older," "I have done more work," "the other is treated better than I." If such thoughts come they should be quickly cut off. If you dwell on them or begin to speak about them, the result is a pestilence from which great evils arise.

(*W* 12.4)

You should run a thousand miles from such expressions as: "I was right." "They had no reason for doing this to me." "The one who did this to me was wrong." God deliver us from this poor way of reasoning. Does it seem to have been right that our good Jesus suffered so many insults and was made to undergo so much injustice?

(*W* 13.1)

Do we think that with vain honors we can imitate Him in the contempt He suffered so that we might reign forever? Such a road leads nowhere; it's the wrong, wrong road; we will never arrive by it.

(*L* 27.13)

Never does the world exalt without putting down....I have a lot of experience of this. It used to afflict me to see so much blindness in these praises, and now I laugh at myself as though someone crazy were speaking. Remember your sins, and if in some matters people speak the truth in praising you, note that the virtue is not yours and that you are obliged to serve more. Awaken fear in your soul so that you do not rest in the kiss of this false peace given by the world; think that it is a kiss from Judas;...stand here with a sword in the hand of your thoughts. Although you think the praise does you no harm, do not trust it. Remember how many were at the top and are now at the bottom. There is no security while we are alive. For love of God, always wage an interior war against these praises.

(*SS* 2.13)

When the soul reaches the stage at which it pays little attention to praise, it pays much less to disapproval; on the contrary, it rejoices in this and finds it a very sweet music. This is an amazing truth. Blame does not intimidate the soul but strengthens it. Experience has already taught it the wonderful gain that comes through this path.

(IC 6.1.5)

❖

I have seen through experience the great good that comes to a soul when it does not turn aside from obedience. It is through this practice that I think one advances in virtue and gains humility.... [T]hose restless stirrings within us, which make us fond of doing our own will and which even subdue reason in matters concerning our own satisfaction, come to a stop. Those who practice obedience remember that they resolutely surrendered their own will to God's will, using submission to the one who stands in God's place as a means to this surrender.

(F P.1)

There is no path that leads more quickly to the highest perfection than obedience.... The highest perfection obviously does not consist in interior delights or in great raptures or in visions or in the spirit of prophecy but in having our will so much in conformity with God's will that there is nothing we know He wills that we do not want with all our desire, and in accepting the bitter as happily as we do the delightful when we know that His Majesty desires it. This seems most difficult (not the doing of it, but this being content with what completely contradicts our nature); and indeed it truly is difficult. But love has this strength if it is perfect, for we forget about pleasing ourselves in order to please the one we love. And truly this is so; for even though the trials may be very great, they become sweet when we know we are pleasing to God. And this is the way by which those who have reached this stage love persecutions, dishonor, and offenses.

(F 5.10)

We [religious] cannot be deceived as much as can those who live in their own homes.... [T]here is no one to inform them of their faults. In monasteries I have never seen this lack, for souls must do, not what they want, but what they are told. Instead, people living in their own homes cannot know their own faults.... [E]ven though they may go against their own will sometimes, they do not exercise themselves so much in mortification. Let us exclude some persons to whom our Lord has given light for many years, for these persons seek someone to whom they may submit, and their great humility leads them to have little confidence in themselves, however learned they may be.

(*SS* 2.25)

I should like the five of us who at present love each other in Christ to make a kind of pact that since others in these times gather together in secret against His Majesty to prepare wicked deeds and heresies, we might seek to gather together some time to free each other from illusion and to speak about how we might mend our ways and please God more since no one knows himself as well as others who observe him if they do so with love and concern for his progress. I say we should gather in secret because this kind of talk is no longer in fashion. Even preachers are composing their sermons so as not to displease. They may have good intentions, and the good deeds may follow; but the result is that few try to amend! But why don't sermons influence many to give up public vice? Do you know my opinion? Those who preach are very cautious; they don't have the great fire of love of God that the Apostles did, and so the flame has little power to enkindle.

(*L* 16.7)

Chapter 2

Love and Friendship

How great the consolation to find you are not alone. The two become a powerful help to each other in suffering and meriting. What excellent backing they give to one another.

(*L* 34.16)

Teresa was warm and affectionate and had an extraordinary gift for friendship. A separate volume could be written on Teresa and her friends — men and women, family and benefactors, confessors and advisers, friars and nuns, laypersons and churchmen, nobles and people of little means, and sinners and saints. Teresa's 450 extant letters are written to over one hundred different recipients. Almost eight hundred friends and acquaintances are addressed or mentioned in a remarkable collection.

Other spiritual leaders downplay the role of human friendship. Teresa's good friend, St. Peter of Alcántara, did not look at a woman for many years. For three years he lived in a Franciscan house and never raised his eyes, so he knew the other friars only by their voices. In radical and relieving contrast, Teresa was a born lover and friend and gives us a remarkable portrait of the primacy of friendship along the spiritual path.

Teresa's friendships with women were tender and loving. She called Ana de Jesús "my crown" and Brianda de San José "excellent company." She loved to chat with María Bautista and was "very, very grieved" when they could not visit. Doña Guiomar de Ulloa was as close to her as a sister. Ana de San Bartolomé became her companion the last five years of her life after Teresa broke her arm and needed a nurse and secretary. As Teresa lay dying, Ana remained constantly at her bedside until the insensitive Antonio de Heredia sent her away to eat. In her brief absence, Teresa became disturbed and struggled to find her in the room. When Ana returned, Teresa smiled peacefully, laid her head in Ana's arms, and died there.

The woman Teresa loved most was María de San José, prioress of Seville. Teresa repeatedly called her "my friend" and wrote: "You must not imagine I love anyone more than you.... I sometimes get such longings to see you that I seem able to think of nothing else.... I long to embrace you again and again.... May His Majesty watch over you for me, and let me see you again before I die." (The latter wish was not fulfilled.) Teresa had such high regard for María that she wanted her to become foundress after her death. (This also was not to be.)

Male Friends

Teresa's male friends were even more numerous and intimate. In her writings she calls Don Francisco de Salcedo the *caballero santo*, the "holy gentleman." She never wanted to live without him. "God grant you life until I die," she wrote, "and then I shall ask Our Lord to take you quickly, so that I may not be parted from you in Heaven." Teresa loved to hear from Domingo Báñez and felt sad when she opened a packet of letters and didn't see his writing. "I got so used to having frequent letters from you that I feel lost without them now," she wrote Don Martín Alonso de Salinas. "It will be a tremendous relief to me to have you here," she told her brother Lorenzo, as he prepared to return to Spain after thirty-five years in Ecuador.

Teresa met Gaspar de Salazar, S.J., at a time when she was in dire need of understanding. She usually hated talking about herself. But when she went to see Salazar, they became immediate soul-mates: "I felt in my spirit I don't know what that I never recall having felt with anyone, neither before nor afterward," she wrote in her *Life*. (She had not yet met Gracián.) "For it was a spiritual joy and understanding within my soul that his soul would understand mine and that mine would be in harmony with his." The story of her encounter with García de Toledo, O.P., is strikingly similar.

But the man Teresa clearly loved above all others was Jerónimo Gracián de la Madre de Dios, though he was half her age and knew her only the last seven years of her life. "You make me so very happy!" she told him. "I need you sorely." She often reminisced about their first meeting in Beas in the spring of 1575: "I shall never have a better time than I had there." She even playfully teased him about whether or not he loved her more than his mother.

What about St. John of the Cross, whom history usually associates with St. Teresa? She dearly loved him too, calling him a great treasure, a tower of strength, and the "father of my soul." When he left for southern Spain, Teresa sorely missed their conversations: "I have not found another like him in the whole of Castile." She was concerned that Gracián worked him too hard and warned: "You will have few left like him, if he dies."

The difference in Teresa's love for these two men is not one of quantity but one of tonality, best illustrated by their responses to her letters. Both had to destroy a number of them at the time of the persecution. But what did they do with the rest? John was afraid he was becoming too attached to the ones he carried with him, so he tore them all up. Gracián sewed all of his together into a book and kept them with him until close to his death when he bequeathed them to his sister to preserve for posterity. (He was one of the first to recommend their publication.) John's action indicates why Teresa believed he'd been a saint all his life and Gracián's why she confessed that his love was one of her few earthly consolations.

In 1580 an epidemic of influenza swept though Spain. Teresa was severely afflicted twice that year and survived. But many of her friends died. She lamented: "Why has God left me in the world to see so many of his servants die?" When she had to return to Avila, she said: "I should not be human if I did not feel returning there very keenly, with my brother and my friends gone, and the worst thing is what the people are like who remain." Loneliness in the absence of the beloved is part of the price we pay for the joys of loving.

The Meaning of Love

But what do we mean by love? Out of vast experience Teresa distinguished between two kinds: a purer, more spiritual love and a "mixed" love that involves our passion, sensuality, and self-interest. Very few of us are capable of the purer love. Teresa was one of them, but it was not always so, and she learned the way we all do: through trial and error, unhealthy attachments, mistakes, messiness, and pain.

It isn't easy to distinguish between the two kinds of love. But those who live on a higher spiritual plane love more majestically. They are still moved erotically on the natural level of physical attraction, for not to be would be inhuman. "Yes, it pleases them to see bodies," Teresa admits in all her sensuous womanliness. "But, no, they do not stop there."

This high level of love does not discount the physical but integrates it into a higher selfless concern for the spiritual perfection of the other. Knowing that when we desire love from another we are always seeking our own satisfaction, those who love on the purer level no longer *seek* to be loved by others, yet gratefully rejoice when they are.

Are these people overly spiritualized, interested only in God and not other human beings, and therefore not really warm or loving? Teresa's example shows that they are even greater lovers: "I say, yes they do love, with a much greater and genuine love, and with passion, and with a more beneficial love; in short, it is love." This love is all the more authentic because it seeks to give more than to receive. Although mere chemical attractions have usurped the name "love," only self-oblivious generosity truly merits that name.

The cost of loving this well is high: anxiety, worry, tears, sacrifice, prayer. We rejoice when our friends rejoice, suffer when they suffer. We are never without proper concern for them.

Teresa's life is full of this compassion. She anguished when Alonso Velázquez lost his vision in one eye, urged Bañez to wear more clothes and wrap up his feet, and advised Brianda when she was seriously ill: "I am astounded they are telling you to get up in weather like this. For pity's sake do not do so: it's enough to kill you." She prayed with her friends for the safe deliveries of their babies and grieved with those who lost loved ones. "Put everything into God's hands," she wrote her nephew on the death of his wife, "for His Majesty will do what is best." With the letter she also sent him two melons. She congratulated Avila's Bishop Mendoza on the marriage of his niece and relieved him of his anxiety over the advanced age of the new husband: "Everything cannot be perfect; it would be much more unsuitable if the bridegroom were very young. Women are always taken better care of when their husbands are mature and a girl with such an affectionate nature is sure to be particularly well treated."

Gracián, of course, was a major concern: his health, his workload, his fatigue. At the time of the persecution of the Reform, Teresa's concern escalated dramatically, and with good reason. She feared he might be murdered on the road and urged him to travel by circuitous routes. She worried that he'd be poisoned and arranged to have him eat in the Seville convent. She was sometimes so anxious for him she couldn't even pray. "It has all come upon me at once," she wrote him. "I felt so overcome at seeing you that all yesterday, Wednesday, my heart was aching, for I could not bear to see you worrying so — and quite justifiably — scenting danger in everything and having to go about along byways like a malefactor.... [T]he Lord had looked for a good way of making me suffer by willing that the blows should fall in a place where they will hurt me more than if they fell on me."

Her fears for St. John of the Cross were also strong. The very day after his kidnapping she wrote to the king, begging him to intervene. During the nine months of John's imprisonment, she mentioned him to innumerable correspondents because she feared for his life, because no one seemed to be doing anything, and because she was helpless except for letter-writing. "I am appalled at the way they have spirited off Fray John of the Cross, and at the time this business is taking," she wrote, calling the whole affair "a piteous story."

True lovers compassionately feel the suffering of their friends and would want to take it upon themselves if they could. But at the same time, they recognize the importance of "tough love," grounded in truth and integrity. Real love therefore does not seek only to console and please the beloved, but also to criticize and challenge when necessary. "When I really love anyone, I am so anxious she should not go astray that I become unbearable," Teresa confessed to María de San José. In various letters she gave her "a thoroughly good scolding" for parading her rhetoric, for being "an ungrateful creature," for wanting a new house when her present one was adequate, and for thinking of her own community instead of the whole order. She chided her cousin, María Bautista, prioress of Valladolid, for being rash, vain, self-willed, inflexible, jealous, greedy, persnickety, and too attached to getting her own way: "If you would occasionally believe what I tell you, we should not get into so much trouble. . . . I don't know why you are so foolish."

Even the beloved Gracián came under fire when he deserved it. Teresa challenged him for complaining about minor sufferings ("What if they treated you like John of the Cross?"), for not informing her of his whereabouts ("This would be troublesome if any emergency arose"), and for exercising authority without substantiating it ("something which must never be done for any reason whatsoever"). She tried unsuccessfully for years to help him overcome his major flaw: He was too innocent, naive, and trusting, too easily influenced by others, unable to imagine the deception even his friends were capable of. When he failed to follow her advice to communicate directly and immediately with the Carmelite general at the outset of the persecution, and the general died before any reconciliation, Teresa sadly and severely rebuked Gracián. At one point she told him: "You exasperate me so much that I don't know how I manage to write nicely to you."

Sometimes we must challenge those we love when we see them at fault. But other times we need to ignore these faults, suffer them silently, and not be surprised or shocked by them. Love is often spoiled by excessive zeal and criticism. We must also be careful not to ignore our own faults or make excuses for ourselves. Even though we may be blamed for wrongs we haven't committed, this is often good for us because we are seldom entirely blameless. Teresa actually sought counsel from those she knew did not agree with her. She lists them in the spiritual testimony she made to the Inquisition in Seville. She rejoiced when one of them came to see her and ruthlessly corrected her faults: "This Father Visitor gives me new life, and I do not believe he will have illusions about me, as everyone else has, for God is being pleased to show him how wretched I am, and he is catching me out in imperfections the whole time. This comforts me very much and I see to it that he is fully aware of them."

We see from Teresa's life how much love hurts. She never stopped loving Gracián or the Marías despite the grief they caused her. She was faithful: she never let a new friend replace an old one. Meeting Gracián did not obliterate her love for Salazar. As late as 1577 she wrote to Salazar in Granada: "It would certainly be some small relief to my soul if I had you." Though others became new soul-mates, she remained faithful to Salcedo for over twenty-five years as one of her first: "I might almost go so far as to term him the person to whom ... I owe most in the world, for he was the first who seriously enlightened me." Teresa's heart grew so expansive, there was always room for another love, always room to forgive one who had pained her.

Where did this spaciousness come from? Teresa knew she did not have enough strength to love within herself, a lack we all share. "How little trust one can place in anyone but God," she wrote in her last letter to Gracián. Teresa placed her trust in Christ, for "He is the true friend." "Oh, strong love of God!" she prayed, knowing that her power to love came from the one she truly adored as "the very Lord of love."

Meditation

In the following texts, Teresa shows how our love of God is the real source of our love for others and how real love cannot remain cheap talk but must show itself in deeds. She describes the value of good friendship, her relationship with García de Toledo as an example, and the pain of separation. Then Teresa distinguishes between two types of love, shows how deeper love goes beyond the body, and urges us to overlook the faults of others and focus on our own.

In conclusion, we see Teresa's love letters to María de San José and Don Jerónimo Reinoso and a critical one to María Bautista. Her long letter to Isabel de San Jerónimo and María de San José was written after two sisters, Beatriz and Margarita, upheaved their community with false accusations and then deposed the rightful leader. Teresa's sage advice on forgiving and not reliving the past wounds is clearly applicable to us today in our own pain.

Teresian Texts: Love and Friendship

Be certain that the more advanced you see you are in love for your neighbor the more advanced you will be in the love of God.... [I]f we practice love of neighbor with great perfection, we will have done everything. I believe that, since our nature is bad, we will not reach perfection in the love of neighbor if that love doesn't rise from the love of God as its root.... [L]et's try to understand ourselves even in little things, and pay no attention to any big plans that sometimes suddenly come to us during prayer in which it seems we will do wonders for our neighbor and even for just one soul so that it may be saved. If afterward our deeds are not in conformity with those plans, there will be no reason to believe that we will accomplish the plans.... When I see souls very earnest in trying to understand the prayer they have and very sullen when they are in it — for it seems they don't dare let their

minds move or stir lest a bit of their spiritual delight and devotion be lost — it makes me realize how little they understand
of the way by which union is attained; they think the whole
matter lies in these things. No, Sisters, absolutely not; works
are what the Lord wants! He desires that if you see a Sister who is sick to whom you can bring some relief, you have
compassion on her and not worry about losing this devotion;
and that if she is suffering pain, you also feel it.... This is true
union with His will, and if you see a person praised, the Lord
wants you to be much happier than if you yourself were being praised. This, indeed, is easy, for if you have humility you
will feel sorry to see yourself praised. But this happiness that
comes when the virtues of the Sisters are known is a very good
thing; and when we see some fault in them, it is also a very
good thing to be sorry and hide the fault as though it were
our own.... [I]f we fail in love of neighbor we are lost.... When
you see yourselves lacking in this love, even though you have
devotion and gratifying experiences that make you think you
have reached this stage, and you experience some little suspension in the prayer of quiet (for to some it then appears that
everything has been accomplished), believe me you have not
reached union.... [F]orce your will to do the will of your Sisters in everything even though you may lose your rights; forget
your own good for their sakes no matter how much resistance
your nature puts up; and, when the occasion arises, strive to
accept work yourself so as to relieve your neighbor of it. Don't
think that it won't cost you anything or that you will find everything done for you. Look at what our Spouse's love for us cost
Him.

(IC 5.3.8–12)

If any begin to give themselves to God, there are so many to
criticize them that they need to seek companionship to defend
themselves until they are so strong that it is no longer a burden
for them to suffer this criticism. And if they don't seek this companionship they will find themselves in much difficulty.... For in
falling I had many friends to help me; but in rising I found my-

self so alone that I am now amazed I did not remain forever
fallen.

(L 7.22)

While I was there it happened that a certain religious came to
that city, a person from the nobility with whom I had sometimes conversed many years previously [García de Toledo].
Once, when attending Mass at a monastery of his order near
the place where I was staying, there came over me a desire to
know the condition of his soul since I wanted him to be a great
servant of God; and I rose to go to speak to him. Since I was
already recollected in prayer, it seemed to me after I got up that
it was a waste of time, and I wondered why I should meddle,
and returned to my seat. It seems to me that this happened
three times, and finally, the good angel was more powerful
than the bad; I went to call him, and he came to speak with me
in the confessional. We began to question each other — for it
was many years since we had met — about our lives. I began
to tell him I had experienced many trials of soul. He strongly
urged me to tell him what the trials were. I told him they were
not meant to be known nor was it meant that I should speak of
them. He said that since the Dominican Father I mentioned —
who was a great friend of his — knew about them he would find
out from him and that I shouldn't worry about it.

The fact is that neither was it in his power to stop press-
ing me nor was it in mine, it seems to me, to resist speaking
about them. For despite all the displeasures and shame I usually felt when I spoke about these things, I didn't feel any pain
with him or with the rector I mentioned [Gaspar de Salazar];
rather, I was very much consoled. I told him about them under
the seal of confession. He seemed to me wiser than ever, although I always thought he had a great mind. I considered the
wonderful talents and gifts he had for doing much good, were
he to give himself totally to God. I've experienced this for some
years: as soon as I see a person who greatly pleases me, with
longings I sometimes cannot bear, I want to see him give himself totally to God. And although I desire that all serve God, the

longings come with very great impulses in the case of these persons I like; so I beg the Lord very much on their behalf. With the religious I'm speaking of, it so happened to me.

He asked me to pray earnestly to God for him, but he had no need to ask since I was already of such a mind that I couldn't have done otherwise. I went to the place where I usually prayed alone and, being deeply recollected, began to talk to the Lord in a foolish way, which I often do without knowing what I'm saying. It is love that is then speaking, and the soul is so transported that I don't notice the difference there is between it and God. Love that knows it possesses His Majesty forgets the soul and thinks it is in Him and, as one without division, speaks absurdities. I recall that after having begged Him with many tears for that soul, that it be truly committed to His service, I said that even though I considered him good this didn't satisfy me, since I wanted him to be very good; and so I said to His Majesty: "Lord, You must not deny me this favor; see how this individual is fit to be our friend."

(*L* 34.6–8)

To leave my daughters and sisters when going from one place to another, was not the smallest cross, I tell you, since I love them so much; especially when I thought I was not going to return to see them again and I saw their great sadness and tears. Even though they are detached from other things, God has not given them the gift to be detached from me, perhaps so that it might be a greater torment to me, for I am not detached from them either, even though I forced myself as much as I could so as not to show it and I reprimanded them. But this was of little help since their love for me is great, and in many ways it is obvious that this love is true.

(*F* 27.18)

❖

Two kinds of love are what I'm dealing with: one kind is spiritual, because it in no way seems to stir sensuality or affect the tenderness of our nature so as to take away purity. The other is spiritual mixed with our sensuality and weakness or good love, for it seems to be illicit, as is love for our relatives and friends.... The love that is spiritual... is not affected by any passion; where passion is present the good order is thrown into complete disorder.

(*W* 4.12–13)

As soon as these persons love, they go beyond the bodies and turn their eyes to the soul and look to see if there is something to love in the soul. And if there isn't anything lovable, but they see something beginning and readiness so that if they love this soul and dig in this mine they will find gold, their labor causes them no pain. Nothing could be presented to them that they wouldn't eagerly do for the good of this soul, for they desire to continue loving it; but they know that if it does not love God very much and have His blessings, their loving it is impossible.

(*W* 6.8)

Let us look at our own faults and leave aside those of others, for it is characteristic of persons with such well ordered lives to be shocked by everything. Perhaps we could truly learn from the one who shocks us what is most important even though we may surpass him in external composure and our way of dealing with others. Although good, these latter things are not what is most important; nor is there any reason to desire that everyone follow at once our own path, or to set about teaching the way of the spirit to someone who perhaps doesn't know what such a thing is. For with these desires that God gives us... about the good of souls, we can make many mistakes.

(*IC* 3.2.13)

❖

Jesus be with your Reverence, my daughter. You will certainly have had a good Christmas and New Year as you have my Father with you; if I had had him, I should have had one too. But it seems unlikely that affairs your way will finish very soon and I am suffering just now from the isolation we feel so much at

Toledo. Oh, what frosts we get here! It is almost as bad as at Avila; and yet I am well, though I long to see a letter from one of you — it seems such a time since I had one last. The couriers, too, are as slow in coming to us as in going to you. But the fact is, things always seem to come slowly when you are longing for them.

I saw from the note on the cover of your letter that you have been better since you were bled, but what I want to know is if your fever has gone. I was delighted to get your letter and I should be more so still if I could see you. It would give me a special and particular happiness just now, for I think we should be very close to each other. There are few women with whom I should like to discuss so many things, for talking to you gives me real pleasure; so I am very glad now to understand from your letters that we have understood each other; and, if God should grant us to meet again, you would not be foolish this time, for you have realized now that I love you, which is the reason why I feel so tenderly for you in your illness.

(*Le* 159 to María de San José)

May the grace of the Holy Spirit be with you. I am back in Avila, my Father, and would gladly be your daughter again if you were here, for I feel very lonely in this place and have no one to turn to for comfort. God help me — the farther I journey in this life, the less comfort I find.

I was not well when I arrived here, as I had got something or other which gave me a touch of fever. I am all right now, and seem to be enjoying some bodily relief, now that I shall not have to do any more travelling yet awhile. I assure you these journeys are dreadfully tiring, though I cannot say I thought the journey from Palencia to Soria so. In fact, it quite refreshed me, for the road was level and often had river views which I found most companionable. Our good prebendary will have told you what we suffered on our journey here.

It is a strange thing that no one who tries to show me kindness escapes severe trials; still, God gives them the charity to be glad of it as He has you. Be sure you do not fail to write me a line when you have anyone to send it by, trying though you may find it, for I can tell you I get very little relaxation and have many troubles.

I was glad to hear Dionisia had entered (the convent). Please tell her relative, the chief courier, and send her a kind message from me. And do not forget to commend me to God.

As I came here so recently, I have no lack of visitors, so I have little time to seek relief in writing to you.

(*Le* 378 to Don Jerónimo Reinoso)

Your Reverence must not be so clever.... [Y]ou must not suppose you will find just what you want everywhere.... It is a great mistake to think you know everything, and then say you are humble. You do not look beyond the limits of your own small house, whereas you should be considering what is most important for the houses as a whole. To do that is to lay the foundations of unrest and to bring everything toppling to the ground.... A fine thing it would be if we embarked upon a project, and then had to abandon it just because your Reverence is so inflexible in your standards. No other prioress has ever taken up such an attitude to me — nor has anyone who is not a prioress either. To do such a thing, I assure you, would be tantamount to losing my friendship.

You know I dislike the way all of you (at Valladolid) think no one can see things as your Reverence can: that, as I say, is because you are concerned only with your own community and not with things that affect many other communities as well. As if it were not enough that you should be self-willed yourself, you have to teach the other nuns to be so too. Perhaps that nun (you reject) will be holier than any other. I cannot think where you get so much vanity from to give you all that rashness.

(*Le* 78A to María Bautista)

I loved you all dearly as it was, but I love you twice as much now, especially your Reverence, who has been the chief sufferer....

Little truth has been spoken lately in your convent and it grieved me deeply to hear the things that were said when they brought those charges against you. Some of them, I knew, were completely false, as I was with you when they were supposed to have happened. Now that I have seen what those nuns have been doing I have given Our Lord hearty thanks that He did not allow them to bring up anything worse.

Those two souls have filled me with dismay: we must all offer very special prayers that God will give them light. I have been apprehensive of what has now happened ever since Father Garciálvarez began to behave in that way, and, if your Reverence remembers, I told you in two of my letters that I believed that there was trouble brewing inside the community. I even named one of the nuns — I never realized that Margarita was in it — and warned you to be on your guard; for, as a matter of fact, I was always dissatisfied with her spiritual condition, though sometimes I thought that was because I was so wicked myself and was yielding to temptation. I even discussed it with Father-Master Gracián, who had had a great deal to do with her, in order that he could be on the look-out. So it has been no great surprise to me — not that I thought she was bad, merely a weak-minded person who had been led astray: she was just ripe to be tricked by the devil, as she has been, for he is very good at taking advantage of temperamental and unintelligent people. So we must not blame her so much as be very sorry for her. And your Reverence and all of you must do me the kindness of not departing from what I am about to say to you: believe me, I really think what I suggest will be best....

The first thing I want to say is that you must commend her to His Majesty very earnestly in all your prayers — pray for her every moment of the day, if you can: that is what we shall do here, so that He may grant us the favor of giving her light.... In some ways I look upon her as a person out of her mind. You see, I know of certain persons, though not in any of our houses, whose imagination is so unstable that they think they really see everything that comes into their minds.... So perhaps she is not so much to blame as we thought she was, just as no blame attaches to a madman who really gets it into his head that he is God the Father so that nothing will drive the idea out again. Your love for God, my sisters, must show itself in your pity for her, which must be as great as though she were as much the daughter of your own father as she is of our true Father, to Whom we owe so much and Whom the poor creature has wanted to serve all her life. Pray, sisters, pray for her, for many of the saints have fallen and then become saints again. Perhaps she needed this experience to humble her, for if God, of His goodness to us, grants her to realize what she has done and to retract it, we shall all have gained through suffering, and she may gain too, for the Lord knows how to bring good out of evil....

And be very careful not to talk about the thing just now; do not even think of it if you can avoid doing so.

The third thing is that you must not show the two sisters any sort of enmity: in fact you should treat the chief culprit more kindly than before, and you must all be kind and sisterly to her, and to the other nun as well. Try to forget what has happened, and think, each of you, how you would like to be treated if it had happened to you. No one may realize it, but believe me, she will be suffering agonies in her soul....

You must not say a word of this in front of her mother, whom I have been very sorry for. Why has no one told me how she has been bearing all these things and what she has said to Beatriz? I have been wanting to know about that and if she has realized what a schemer she has been....

Be very careful not to let the two nuns have a lot of private conversation together. But do not put any strain upon them — for we women are weak till the Lord begins to do His work in us. It would not be a bad idea to keep Beatriz occupied by giving her some duty to perform.... If she is alone, and allowed to think all the time, it will be very bad for her, so if any of the nuns see they can do her good, let them sometimes spend some time with her.

I expect I shall be seeing Father Nicolao before he goes to Seville. I wish it might be soon. We shall then be able to discuss everything in detail. For the present, please do just what I ask you. In any case, those who have a real desire to suffer never bear rancor against those who do them wrong — they only love them the more. You will be able to tell by this if you have all profited by your period of trial. I hope in Our Lord that He will soon put everything right and that the house will be just as it was before, or even better, for His majesty always gives a hundredfold.

Now mind, I ask you once again very earnestly not on any account to talk among yourselves about the past: it can do you no good and may do a great deal of harm.

(*Le* 274 to Isabel de San Jerónimo
and María de San José)

Chapter 3

Man and Woman

Oh, Jesus, how wonderful it is when two souls understand each other!
(*Le* 146 to Gracián)

Teresa deeply appreciated both men and women, as we have seen in her friendships. At the same time, she was highly critical of the dark or shadow side of both masculine and feminine. In her major writings, Teresa openly critiques women for both their strengths and their weaknesses, though never systematically. Her critique of men is no less impassioned, and it appears more in her life and letters.

"Just being a woman is enough to have my wings fall off," she wrote. She uses the adjectives "womanly" and "womanish" negatively. In a long list of what's wrong with her, she concludes (referring to herself in the third person): "In sum, she is a woman" — as though all that went before did not have to be mentioned, but only her gender. She points out that women are excessive — in their devotions, which can be "foolish" and "superstitious"; in their loving, which leads to attachments; in their penances; and in their sensitivities. They complain too much about their "little illnesses." Therefore they must not be treated softly, but firmly.

Women are very susceptible to illusions, and this is dangerous. In Teresa's view, human nature is already weak, but especially in women. This makes women prone to hysteria and false mysticism, inclined to believe that everything is a rapture or an ecstasy. "It seems to me common sense to flee from the tongue of a passionate woman as one would from a wild beast," Teresa wrote to a Jesuit friend. "I know only too well what a great many women are like when they are all together," she said. "Believe me, I am more afraid of a discontented nun than of a horde of devils." Teresa's overarching criticism of women, however, is for their weakness and lack of courage. "Those who are pusillanimous and weak in spirit — for the most part will be women." When she speaks of courage, she makes it clear that this is "certainly not a characteristic of women." In a letter to Gracián she wrote: "Women are like that — timorous creatures, most of them." For this reason she tells her sisters: "I would not want you to be womanish in anything, nor would I want you to be like women but like strong men. For if you do what lies in your power, the Lord will make you so strong that you will astonish men."

Teresa apologizes for being a woman and equates her femininity with weakness. She calls herself useless, little, helpless, poor, "weak and with hardly any fortitude." Did she really believe this? Or was she simply using a coy tactic to get past her censors and avoid the Inquisition in an era when women were considered radically inferior? For the most part, Teresa truly *did* believe her analysis of women because she was humbly aware of her own shadow. But there are also times when she seems to be calling herself a "poor little woman" tongue-in-cheek, with a rakish wink and a wry smile.

Teresa is not guilty of gross generalization. She knew there were definitely exceptions to her analysis of female weakness. Despite her own timorous periods, she also said: "I am not at all like a woman,... for I have a robust spirit." She knew she had more courage than most women. The women who joined her Reform were also strong. She gives them high praise in her letters and her *Foundations.*

Teresa extols women for their many positive qualities. More women than men enjoy extraordinary mystical experience — the angelic side of proneness to illusion. Teresa learned this from St. Peter of Alcántara (by now willing to look a woman in the eye), but she had already observed it herself: "Women make much more progress along this path than men do." Alcántara gave "excellent reasons for this, all in favor of women," Teresa continues, "but there's no need to mention them here." How unfortunate!

Women pay more attention to important little details than men do. They can communicate with each other more easily than men do with one another. Women may even have more or better experience than men in some areas. God may make "a little old woman wiser" in the science of mysticism than a young learned man, Teresa exclaims passionately, out of her frustration over the limitations put on her as a woman.

Teresa was highly critical of marriage. Though she was not initially eager to become a nun, she feared marriage as well. She had seen how it crushed her own mother and robbed her of youth and vitality. She agreed that it was demeaning to be subject to someone in marriage — "to a man who is often the death of [us] and who could also be, God forbid, the death of [our] souls." She speaks compassionately about women in unhappy marriages who suffer because they cannot voice their complaints for fear of annoying their husbands. She goes so far as to tell her nuns to rejoice because they have been freed from such subjection.

This view of the dark side of marriage for women is realistic. But in our own day, we must notice that husbands, because of the emancipation of women, can also be demeaned by being subject to their wives, who are often the death of them and, "God forbid, the death of their souls." This must have been true even in Teresa's time, though not so noticeably. Our contemporary emphasis on mutual respect and partnership is healthy and long overdue.

One of Teresa's friends was ignored by her parents because she was born female into a family of four daughters. This sends Teresa into a scathing tirade against fathers and mothers who overrate their sons and undervalue their daughters: "How many fathers and mothers will be seen going to hell because they had sons and also how many will be seen in heaven because of their daughters."

She envies men who work in the world and feels frustrated because she cannot translate her concerns into heroic deeds: "I

realized I was a woman and incapable of doing any of the use-
ful things I desired to do in the service of the Lord." She longs
to enter the fray and play more of a part in getting people to acknowledge their blindness and turn to God. But when she tries,
"a thousand persecutions rain down" on her, and she is criticized for wanting to teach the men from whom she should be
learning, a desire revealing a lack of humility.

As always, her humor saves her, and she makes fun of herself. By the time Teresa wrote *The Way of Perfection,* however, her
frustration level peaked, and she penned a potent paragraph
lambasting the "sons of Adam" for undervaluing women and
holding them suspect. García de Toledo deleted this paragraph
in the first redaction of the *Way* because he found it too outrageous for his day. Teresa humbly complied and removed the
passage, now included in contemporary translations. No doubt
all Teresa suffered in her own life has helped bring about the
freedom women enjoy in our world today.

This leads to Teresa's criticism of men. They, too, are excessive, but unlike women in matters of the heart, men are
excessive in matters of the mind. Teresa highly prized the use
of reason, particularly as an antidote to illusory mysticism. But
she criticizes men for being so excessively rational that their
mystical life remains underdeveloped. She challenges "learned
men" — her term for theologians — to put their learning aside
at prayer, to stop searching for ideas, composing speeches, and
using "rhetorical artifices" because "one act of humility is worth
more than all the knowledge of the world." Study is helpful before and after prayer but can make an actual period of
prayer tepid because it inundates the mind with words. Mystical prayer, as we shall see, is not a prayer of many words
but of longing. "It annoys me," Teresa writes, when "men of
prominence, learning, and high intelligence make so much fuss
because God doesn't give them devotion," when devotion is
actually hampered by their attachment to learning.

Men must let go of excessive intellectualizing and be more
open to experience. They are often trapped in the Third Mansion: "Their reason is still very much in control. Love has not yet

reached the point of overwhelming reason." What do men need to let go? A touch of madness — that very quality contemporary men are too apt to dismiss as female hysteria. In her discussion of the Sixth Mansion, Teresa speaks of a "blessed madness" and prays: "If only God would give it to us all!" Why do we need the madness of letting go? Because life is a mystery, and our rational understanding of it is elementary indeed.

One of the great mysteries men will never fathom merely by their use of reason is the mystery of woman. "You must believe that I understand the contradictory ways of women better than you do," she wrote Gracián. "Do believe that I am right in this, and do not forget it if I should die." She has a good laugh at Ambrosio Mariano because he thinks he understands women and wants her to accept a candidate she finds unsuitable: "I was amused at your remark that you could sum her up immediately if you once saw her. We women cannot be summed up as easily as that."

When men do not understand women well enough, they tend to be insensitive, and this leads to emotional abuse and abandonment. Teresa suffered painfully from this, especially toward the end of her life when her male superiors were blind to her weakening condition and pushed her relentlessly. After the persecution of the Reform ended and Teresa needed rest, the acting provincial insisted she travel in cruel weather to make more foundations. Antonio, reveling in his power over her as temporary superior in Gracián's absence, ordered her to Alba de Tormes — the journey that led to her death. Ana de San Bartolomé revealed Teresa's true response: "Never have I seen her suffer from an order given by a superior as she did from this one." But even more painful abuse came from her beloved Gracián.

In her later years, age, exhaustion, and failing health deepened Teresa's need for companionship. The usually sensitive Gracián failed to understand. When he cancelled his plan to accompany her on the journey to Soria, she wrote: "The flesh is weak, and what has happened has made me sadder than I could have wished to be: it has been a great blow to me.... [P]lease

God he who was the cause of your Reverence's departure may have (hurried you off) to better purpose than I suspect." Gracián then scheduled travels of his own that made it impossible for him to see Teresa for the last six months of her life.

Mutuality and Interdependence

Teresa endured many disadvantages not suffered by twentieth-century women. But she enjoyed a major advantage that is often tragically missing from the lives of many women today: as a truly liberated woman, Teresa experienced no rancor toward men. She did not hate them or try to build a life without them. She loved and revered men. She knew she needed them and couldn't live without them.

She needed counsel from the great theologians who guided her spiritual life, most of whom became lifetime friends. She wrote affectionately to Domingo Bañez: "No wonder great things are done for the love of God when my love for Fray Domingo has such force that what he approves, I approve, and what he likes, I like. I don't know where this infatuation of mine is going to stop." She needed Julian of Avila, who offered to be her squire, supporting and protecting her on her many journeys. She needed shrewd business advisers like Antonio Gaytán, whom she trusted enough to make foundations without her presence.

But above all, she needed Gracián to carry on the work of her Reform. She was growing progressively more exhausted because of the overwhelming demands sapping her energies. She desperately needed competent help. She cherished John of the Cross as a saint and spiritual adviser, but he was too lofty for the practicalities of administration. She admits she had disagreements with him over business matters and was "vexed with him." Mariano was too hot-headed. Antonio lusted so much for power and prestige, he made bad judgments and erratically wavered between softness and bursts of severity. But when Teresa met Gracián, she said: "Had I very much desired to ask His Majesty for a person to organize all the things pertaining to the order in these initial stages, I would not have succeeded in asking for all that He in fact gave in Father Gracián." This man was brilliantly gifted and utterly dedicated. He and Teresa were of like minds. She believed they were both called by God to the same dream. She was also weary and frustrated after years of moving from one confessor to another, struggling to decide between their sometimes contradictory advice. She was certain that God had brought Gracián to her as a permanent guide. In one of the more remarkable passages in her *Spiritual Testimonies,* Teresa describes how she vowed to obey this man in everything.

Teresa not only needed Gracián as a spiritual director, confessor, and partner in her life's work. She was more than the Mother Foundress. She was a woman. And she needed a confidant and friend, one she could cherish, someone in whom she could delight and find comfort. Her enemies were suspicious of her love for Gracián, and like today's cynics, gave it a bizarre Freudian twist. Without sufficient integrity, purity, and spiritual sensitivity, we cannot recognize the possibility of such simultaneously passionate and chaste love between man and woman. Yet our world is desperate for a new model of how men and women can love each other without lust, cooperate without competition, and serve one another without subservience. Gracián himself describes the truth of it:

> She loved me most tenderly, and I loved her more than any other mortal creature, even more than my own mother. But this great love which I felt for Mother Teresa, and she for me, is of a far different kind from what commonly passes for love in this world, for that is fraught with danger and gives rise to unholy thoughts and temptations which bring no solace but rather weaken spiritual fervor and arouse sensuality. But this love of mine for Mother Teresa, and hers for me, engendered in me purity, spirituality, and love of God, and brought her consolation and relief in her trials, as she often told me herself, and so she would not have my own mother love me more than she did.

As Teresa recognized the need for men in her life, she also knew that the men in her life needed her. Her impact on men of stature is all the more remarkable in a culture that did not appreciate the contribution of women. She persuaded John of the Cross to join the Carmelite Reform instead of the Carthusians and instructed him personally in her new way of life. She gave spiritual advice to Don Teutonio Braganza, archbishop of Evora, the first to publish *The Way of Perfection*. She served as spiritual director to her wealthy and worldly brother Lorenzo. "He would tell me everything, and it was extraordinary what trust he placed in the things I said to him." When the duke of Alba, captain general of the Netherlands, fell into disfavor with the king, the burden of his imprisonment was lightened by reading Teresa's *Life*. Dr. Pedro Castro y Nero, a prominent theologian, was prepared to discredit Teresa's writings. But he found himself so entranced, he confessed that no devotional book ever moved him more than Teresa's. Both times Teresa was denounced to the Inquisition, her judges responded this same positive way.

The Carmelite father general in Rome admitted that Teresa did more good for the order than all the Carmelite friars in Spain. All the friars needed Teresa. But Gracián, in view of his leadership, needed her most of all. "She so captivated me," he admitted, "that from that moment (I first met her) I did nothing of importance without first consulting her." Unfortunately he did not always follow her sage advice.

Teresa and the men in her life needed one another — not as functionaries to *do for* each other, though there certainly was a great deal of mutual assistance. More importantly, Teresa and her male friends needed one another as persons to *be with* each other, complementary companions on the spiritual quest. Like us, Teresa was always in search of soul-mates. She found them — in Salcedo, Salazar, García de Toledo, and Domingo Bañez. In December 1574, she wrote sadly to Bañez: "I do not think this world can give me any comforts now; for I have not got what I want and I do not want what I have. The trouble is that what used to give me such comfort in my confessors does so no longer. A priest must be more than a confessor to me now. The soul's desire can only be assuaged by some other soul which understands it." Three months later she met her ultimate soul-mate in Gracián and rejoiced in their "fellow-feeling." As she wrote him: "Oh, Jesus, how wonderful it is when two souls understand each other! They never lack anything to say and never grow weary (of saying it)." Many of us never find our real soul-mate because we become distracted by those who far more easily become mere "body-mates."

Emotional Addiction

Teresa's life experience was rich enough for her to realize that man-woman friendships are not always positive. In our own day, we use the words "co-dependency" and "emotional addiction" to describe one kind of problem that arises between men and women. In Teresa's time, this problem was called attachment, inordinate friendship, or excessive love. Teresa was deeply concerned about it, for it threatened not only the freedom of her followers but her own freedom as well. Until her early forties, Teresa herself was prone to attachment to men.

What do we mean by emotional addiction? Teresa calls it a "shackle" and "a chain that cannot be broken by any file." It is natural to be "inclined to one more than another," but we must be careful not to allow ourselves to be *dominated* by that affection. An attachment enslaves us, robbing us of our freedom. "Oh, God help me," Teresa raves, "the silly things that come from such attachment are too numerous to be counted." Through an attachment our affections become excessively "involved" — like children in their games.

Teresa became overinvolved — "enmeshed," as we say today — many times in her early life, compromising her integrity, losing her freedom, dispersing her energy. The first instance occurred at age sixteen when she fell in love with one of her cousins. The next occurred at age twenty-four, around the time she went to the *curandera*, the herbal folk healer, in Becedas. Her

severe illness had not marred her beauty, and as she confessed
to the local parish priest, he fell in love with her. In her *Life*,
Teresa tells us how strongly he loved her: "His affection for me
was not bad; but since it was too great, it came to no good." This
is one of the most intriguing episodes in Teresa's life.

The priest began to bare his soul to her: For seven years
he had kept a concubine, and the whole town knew it. He lost
his honor and reputation, and no one dared confront him. The
woman kept her hold on him through the charms she put in a
copper idol and asked him to wear around his neck.

Teresa courageously confronted the man and convinced him
to give her the idol, which she threw into a river. The priest
awoke as if from a deep sleep, came to his senses, and stopped
seeing the woman. He never tired of thanking God for showing
him the light and died exactly one year from the day he first met
Teresa. A dramatic conversion story with a virtuous ending. So
why did it still disturb Teresa when she wrote about it almost
twenty-five years later?

She recognized her inordinate emotional involvement with
the man. She accused herself of being frivolous, blind, and un-
duly moved by the fact that he loved her: "Damned be such
loyalty that goes against the law of God!" she wrote with more
than her usual vehemence. She admitted that the priest's affection for her could have been purer and confessed even more
humbly: "There were also occasions on which, if we had not remained very much in God's presence, there would have been
more serious offenses." Her intention in loving him was good,
she knew, but the deed bad: "For in order to do good, no matter
how great, one should not commit the slightest wrong."

Some years later, Teresa's head was turned again by the vanity of being loved — in the parlor of the Monastery of the Incarnation, where she became the center of attraction. Her *Life*
is truly discreet here, and she refers simply to "a person," but
evidence strongly suggests another man. "No other friendship
was as much a distraction to me as this one," Teresa admits,
"for I was extremely fond of it." Blinded once again by love,
it took a vision of Christ, looking at her with great severity, to

make Teresa "see" her folly. But she was still too weak to make the break. So God sent another warning — this time more amusing. When Teresa was with "this same person" again, they saw a hideous toad moving quickly in their direction. Teresa could not understand how such a repulsive creature could have been there in the middle of the day. There was a great mystery about it, but she clearly understood the message: God was warning her again about another inordinate attachment.

Teresa was trapped because these relationships were not overtly bad. "The attachments didn't seem to me to be improper," she says in her defense. "I was not offending God by them.... It seemed to me it would be ingratitude to abandon them." Most of her confessors agreed, and so they were little help. If they had alerted Teresa to her danger, she would have avoided the friendships and remedied the matter. "The whole trouble," she came to understand, "lay in not getting at the root of the occasions."

Teresa finally found a more challenging confessor. Because she was still fragile, he knew he couldn't force her to give up her addictive behavior. So he advised her to commend the matter to God for some days, pray the hymn *Veni Creator* (Come, Holy Spirit), and beg God to enlighten her. Teresa was in her early forties. She prayed the hymn fervently and experienced her first rapture. Deep within her spirit she heard the words: "No longer do I want you to converse with men but with angels." These words were fulfilled. Teresa changed and abandoned her superficial attachments with courage and freedom, focusing solely on deeper friendships based on the mutual desire for spiritual perfection.

"Well and good," we may say. "If God were to give me a vision or a rapture, I'd give up my attachments, too." But if we were to ponder this more honestly, would we not have to admit that God has indeed enraptured us? Shown us the severity of the divine gaze? Perhaps even sent a toad to warn us?

As in Teresa's case, the chain of an attachment cannot be broken by any file but only by God through our prayer and earnest cooperation. Have we earnestly cooperated? This may mean a careful effort to break away from these friendships. As Teresa sagaciously advises, this must be done delicately and lovingly rather than harshly. But it must be done. Spiritual growth does not mean loving excessively and exclusively but universally and freely: "All must be friends, all must be loved, all must be held dear."

In her loves and friendships, Teresa manifested remarkable universality and freedom. She was never limited to one love or locked into rigid role-playing. Sometimes she was the strong commanding leader — even in relation to men who were significantly older and more learned than she. Sometimes, even at the height of her sanctity, she was genuinely and poignantly the weak one, a "poor little woman," desperately reaching out to men who were much younger. Teresa loved men freely in a fluidity of roles. She was sometimes more dominant, as mother to son, and sometimes more submissive, as daughter to father. García de Toledo was humble enough to call himself her son. At the same time, Teresa called him father because she entrusted him with her soul. There were also many times when Teresa related to men as equals — friend to friend. And she often came as close to relating as lover as is chastely possible for a holy, celibate woman.

All this occurred in an atmosphere of mutual respect and appreciation. As a result, we see an incomparable spark and richness that erupt from the unique man-woman dynamic. Teresa became more womanly as a result of her love for men. The men in her life became more manly as a result of her love for them. The nature of man and the nature of woman cannot unfold except in relation to each other. Here is where we discover true feminine and masculine strength. Only the weak and unintegrated woman tries to go it alone without acknowledging her need for men. Only the weak and unintegrated man ignores his need for women on the deepest levels of life that transcend superficial sexuality. This balance may well be Teresa's most crucial contribution to a modern world crippled simultaneously by male-bashing and the exploitation of women.

Meditation

In the following texts, Teresa expresses her frustration over being a woman, unable to be more actively involved in the world. She also expresses pain over the subjection of women in marriage. Then she exhorts women to be more courageous and men to appreciate women on a deeper level. After describing the richness of "holy madness," which helps us pursue heroic deeds out of love for Christ, she critiques educated men without experience who think they know more than uneducated women with vast experience.

The next passages are lengthy and touching. We read the intimate details of Teresa's vision of God's act of uniting her life to Gracián's and of her subsequent and difficult vow of obedience to Gracián. We are privileged to see this — Teresa originally intended it to be kept secret. She called it "material having to do with my conscience and soul" and said: "Let no one read it even though I be dead, but give it to the Father Master Gracián." Teresa's initial admiration for this man is tragically juxtaposed with her last correspondence with him, written only one month before her death. Teresa is so disturbed over his carelessness toward her, she has even lost the desire to write him.

The texts on emotional addiction begin with a strong statement on the value of spiritual companionship and conversation, tempered by realistic awareness of the possibility of attachment. Using the example of her enmeshment with the priest in Becedas, Teresa warns against a false loyalty to friends that is really excessive love and enslavement. Then she describes the vision of Christ that helped her break her own inordinate attachments; this is followed by a good analysis of the tendency toward emotional addiction and the Christic focus we need to overcome it. Finally, Teresa indicates her ultimate freedom in friendships and gives a solid spiritual basis for evaluating our own.

Teresian Texts: Man and Woman

The trouble is that for persons as useless as myself there are few opportunities to do something. May you be pleased, my God, that there come a time in which I may be able to repay You even one mite of all I owe You. Ordain, Lord, as You wish, how this servant of Yours may in some manner serve You. Others were women, and they have done heroic things for love of You. I'm not good at anything but talk, and so You don't desire, my God, to put me to work; everything adds up to just words and desires about how much I must serve.... [O]rdain ways in which I might do something for You, for there is no longer anyone who can suffer to receive so much and not repay anything. Cost what it may, Lord, do not desire that I come into Your presence with hands so empty, since the reward must be given in conformity with one's deeds. Here is my life, here is my honor and my will. I have given all to You, I am Yours, make use of me according to Your will. I see clearly, Lord, the little I'm capable of.

(L 21.5)

A woman in this stage of prayer is distressed by the natural hindrance there is to her entering the world, and she has great envy of those who have the freedom to cry out and spread the news abroad about who this great God of hosts is.... Oh, poor little butterfly, bound by so many chains which do not let you fly where you would like!... Let Your grandeur appear in a creature so feminine and lowly.... [S]he would give a thousand lives — if she had that many — if one soul were to praise You a little more through her; and she would consider such lives very well spent.

(IC 6.6.3–4)

On occasion I laugh at myself, and at other times I grow weary. An interior stirring incites me to some service — I'm not capable of any more: arranging branches and flowers before holy images, sweeping, or putting a chapel in order, doing such lowly little things that it embarrasses me.... [W]ere it not for the fact that the Lord accepted my desire, I saw that it had no importance — and I myself made fun of myself.

(*L* 30.20)

They say that for a woman to be a good wife toward her husband she must be sad when he is sad, and joyful when he is joyful, even though she may not be so. (See, what subjection you have been freed from, Sisters!) The Lord, without deception, truly acts in such a way with us. He is the one who submits, and He wants you to be the lady with authority to rule; He submits to your will.

(*W* 26.4)

Those who are pusillanimous and weak in spirit — for the most part they will be women.... [T]heir weak nature fears. It's necessary for us to be on guard because this natural weakness will make us lose a great crown. When you feel this pusillanimity, have recourse to faith and humility, and don't fail to go on fighting with faith, for God can do all. Thus he was able to give fortitude to many saintly girls, and He gave it so that they were able to suffer many torments, since they were determined to suffer for Him.

(*SS* 3.5)

It seems bold that I think I could play some role in obtaining answers to these petitions.... Nor did You, Lord when You walked in the world, despise women; rather, You always, with great compassion, helped them. (And You found as much love and more faith in them than You did in men. Among them was Your most blessed Mother.... Is it not enough, Lord, that the world has intimidated us... so that we may not do anything worthwhile for You in public or dare speak some truths that we lament over in secret, without Your also failing to hear so just a petition?... Since the world's judges are sons of Adam and all of them men, there is no virtue in women that they do not hold suspect.... [T]hese are times in which it would be wrong to undervalue virtuous and strong souls, even though they are women.)

(W 3.7)

✦

How rich he will find that he is, he who has left all riches for Christ! How honored will he be, he who has not sought honor from Him but has enjoyed seeing himself humbled! How wise will he be, he who rejoiced to be considered mad because that is what they called Wisdom Himself! How few madmen there are now — on account of our sins! Truly it seems that now there are no more of those whom people considered mad for doing the heroic deeds of true lovers of Christ.

(L 27.14)

This is a mistake we make: we think with years we shall come to understand what in no way can be comprehended without experience. And so many are wrong, as I said, in wanting to discern spirits without having experience. I don't say that anyone who has not had spiritual experience, provided he is a learned man, should not guide someone who has. But he ought to limit himself to seeing to it that in both exterior and interior matters the soul walks in conformity to the natural way through the use of reason; and in supernatural experiences he should see that it walks in conformity with Sacred Scripture. As for the rest he shouldn't kill himself or think he understands what he doesn't, or suppress the spirit; for now, in respect to the spirit, another greater Lord governs them; they are not without a Superior. . . . Let him not be surprised or think these things are impossible — everything is possible with the Lord — but strive to strengthen his own faith and humble himself in that the Lord makes a little old woman wiser, perhaps in this science than he is, even though he is a very learned man. With this humility he will do more good for souls and for himself than by becoming a contemplative without it. For I repeat that if he doesn't have experience and a very great deal of humility in knowing that he doesn't understand the experience, but that it's not impossible on that account, he will be of little profit to himself and of still less profit to those with whom he deals.

(L 34.11–12)

✣

In 1575, during the month of April, while I was at the foundation in Beas, it happened that the Master Friar Jerome Gratian of the Mother of God came there. I had gone to confession to him at times, but I hadn't held him in the place I had other confessors, by letting myself be completely guided by him. One day while I was eating, without any interior recollection, my soul began to be suspended and recollected in such a way that I thought some rapture was trying to come upon me; and a vision appeared with the usual quickness, like a flash of lightning.

It seemed to me our Lord Jesus Christ was next to me in the form in which He usually appears, and at His right side stood Master Gratian himself, and I at His left. The Lord took our right hands and joined them and told me He desired that I take this master to represent Him as long as I live, and that we both agree in everything because it was thus fitting....

I felt assurance from the vision that such an action suited me, and also comfort coming from the thought that this going about consulting different minds with different opinions was now to end. For some, by not understanding me, made me suffer very much; although I never gave up any of them until either they moved away or I did, because I thought the fault was mine. Twice more the Lord returned to tell me in different words not to fear since He gave Master Gratian to me. So I resolved not to do otherwise, and I made the proposal within myself to carry out the Lord's request for the rest of my life, to follow Father Gratian's opinion in everything as long as it wasn't clearly offensive to God — and I was certain it would not be; for, according to some things I have heard, I believe he has made the same promise I have made, of doing the more perfect thing in all matters.

I was left with a peace and comfort so great I was amazed, and I felt certain the Lord wanted this.... [O]n the other hand it struck me as something very arduous.... [T]his promise would mean remaining without any freedom either interiorly or exteriorly throughout life. And I felt pressed a little, and even very much, not to go through with it.... [T]he difficulty so bothered me I don't think I did anything in my life, not even in making profession, over which I felt within myself greater resistance, except when I left my father's house to become a nun....

At the end of a period of battle, the Lord gave me great confidence so that it seemed to me I made that promise for the Holy Spirit, and that the Spirit was obliged to give the father light so that he in turn might give it to me. It also seemed I was to recall that it was our Lord Jesus Christ who had given me the light. And at this point I knelt down and promised that for the rest of my life I would do everything Master Gratian might tell me....

Although I feared I might be restricted, I was left with greater freedom; and I was more confident our Lord would grant Father Gratian new favors for this service I rendered to God and that I might share in them and receive light in everything.

Blessed be He who created a person who so pleased me that I could dare do this.

(*T* 36)

May the grace of the Holy Spirit be with your Reverence. Your frequent letters to me do not suffice to alleviate my distress, though it was a great relief to me to know you are well and the south is free from sickness. God grant this may continue. As far as I know I have had all your letters.

The reasons you gave for your decision to go did not seem to me sufficient, for you could have found a way of organizing the friars' studies without leaving here.... Then you could have postponed going to the houses in the south for another two months and left the houses here in good order. I cannot think why your Paternity decided to go. So keenly did I feel your being away at such a time that I lost the desire to write to you: so I have not written till to-day, when it is unavoidable. To-day is full moon: I had a perfectly wretched night and my head is bad this morning. Until now I had been better, and to-morrow, when the moon is past the full, I think this indisposition will disappear. The throat trouble is better, but has not yet gone.

I have had a dreadful time here with Don Francisco's mother-in-law. She is a strange woman. She is absolutely bent upon going to law to contest the validity of the will. She is not in the right, of course, but is well thought of, and some people support her, and have advised me to come to an agreement with her, in case Don Francisco should be completely ruined and we should have to pay for it. This will mean a loss to St. Joseph's, but I trust in God that, as its claim is sound, it will eventually inherit everything. I have been pestered to death with it all, and still am, though Teresa has been very good about it. Oh, how sorry she was your Reverence did not come! We have said nothing about it to her until now. In one way I am glad, because she will begin to understand how little trust one can place in anyone but God — and it has done me no harm either.

(*Le* 434 to Gracián)

One day I was wondering if it was an attachment for me to find satisfaction in being with persons with whom I discuss my soul and whom I love, or with those who I see are great servants of God since it consoled me to be with them. The Lord told me that if a sick person who was in danger of death thought a doctor was curing him, that sick person wouldn't be virtuous if he failed to thank and love the doctor; that if it hadn't been for these persons what would I have done; that conversation with good persons is not harmful, but that my words should always be well weighed and holy, and that I shouldn't fail to converse with them; that doing so is beneficial rather than harmful. This consoled me greatly because sometimes, since conversing with them seemed to me to be an attachment, I didn't want to talk to them at all.

(*L* 40.19)

I loved him deeply. I was so frivolous and blind that it seemed to me a virtue to be grateful and loyal to anyone who loved me. Damned be such loyalty that goes against the law of God! This is the kind of nonsense that goes on in the world, which makes no sense to me: that we consider it a virtue not to break with a friendship, even if it go against God, whereas we are indebted to God for all the good that is done to us. Oh blindness of the world!

(*L* 5.4)

Excessive love... carries with it so much evil and so many imperfections.... [T]his excess is hardly noticed by persons having consciences that deal only roughly with pleasing God, and the excess even seems to them virtuous; but those who are interested in perfection have a deep understanding of this excessive love, because little by little it takes away the strength of the will to be totally occupied in loving God.... I believe this excessive love must be found among women even more than among men.

(*W* 4.5–6)

Let us not condescend... to allow our wills to be slaves to anyone, save to the One who bought it with His blood. Be aware that, without understanding how, you will find yourselves so attached that you will be unable to manage the attachment. Oh, God help me, the silly things that come from such attachments are too numerous to be counted.

(*W* 4.8)

While I was once with a person, the Lord at the outset of our acquaintance desired to make me understand that those friendships were not proper for me and to counsel me and give me advice in the midst of such thorough blindness. With great severity, Christ appeared before me, making me understand what He regretted about the friendships. I saw Him with the eyes of my soul more clearly than I could have with the eyes of my body. And this vision left such an impression on me that, though more than twenty-six years have gone by, it seems to me it is still present. I was left very frightened and disturbed, and didn't want to see that person anymore.

(*L* 7.6)

I had a serious fault that did me much harm; it was that when I began to know that certain persons liked me, and I found them attractive, I became so attached that my memory was bound strongly by the thought of them. There was no intention to offend God, but I was happy to see these persons and think about them and about the good things I saw in them. This was something so harmful it was leading my soul seriously astray. After I beheld the extraordinary beauty of the Lord, I didn't see anyone who in comparison with Him seemed to attract or occupy my thoughts. By turning my gaze just a little inward to behold the image I have in my soul, I obtained such freedom in this respect that everything I see here below seems loathsome when compared to the excelling and beautiful qualities I beheld in this Lord. There is no knowledge or any kind of gift that I think could amount to anything when placed alongside of what it is to hear just one word spoken from that divine mouth; how much more so when the words are so many. I hold that it would be impossible for me (provided the Lord would not permit that, on account of my sins, this impression be erased from my memory) to be so occupied with the thought of anyone that I couldn't free myself from it by only a slight effort to remember this Lord.

(*L* 37.4)

I have never again been able to tie myself to any friendship or to find consolation in or bear particular love for any other person than those I understand love Him and strive to serve Him; nor is it in my power to do so, nor does it matter whether they are friends or relatives. If I'm not aware that the person seeks to love and serve God or to speak about prayer, it is a painful cross for me to deal with him.

(*L* 24.6)

Chapter 4

Dare the Dream

Well now how many discreet persons there were who told him his idea was crazy! For those of us who have not reached such love of God, it may seem so. And how much crazier it will be to come to the end of the dream that is this life with so much common sense!

(*SS* 3.8)

Teresa is called the "saint of common sense." But she also knew that we need more than brute practicality and reason if we are to be really alive. We need a dream. All of us have dreams, but many of us never see them come true. What does it take to make a dream a reality? Though Teresa's dream was the reform of a religious order, the stages she experienced are universal.

We can't pinpoint the exact origin of any dream. Who can say how long it gestates in the deepest recesses of the soul before it comes to consciousness? For Teresa, the dream appeared in 1560, as she sat in the Monastery of the Incarnation, presiding over her coterie of relatives and friends. The women discussed the solitary life of the first Carmelite hermits somewhat wistfully, for living as they did in a crowded, bustling convent of 144, where the maximum should have been 60, there was insufficient quiet and recollection for contemplative prayer.

Teresa's young cousin, who later became María Bautista, prioress of Valladolid, was the first to suggest founding a new monastery to imitate the life of the early desert saints. A brave and lofty thought, and an impossible dream, of course — especially for a woman, and one without resources — but Teresa dared the dream. "I have often mentioned this," she said, "and now

I repeat and ask that you always have courageous thoughts. As a result of them the Lord will give you grace for courageous deeds. Believe that these brave thoughts are important." Always convinced of the value of determination, she set to work to make her dream come true.

We must believe in the dream and risk everything to follow it. This usually involves initial daring, which Teresa called "holy audacity." Teresa listened carefully and trusted when God told her this monastery would be "a star shining with great splendor." She took the risk and began even though she had nothing but the dream — no facilities, no money, no support. She signed a contract for a house, drew up plans adapting it for a monastery, and helped supervise construction and mollify the workers when there were no wages to pay them. She knew that the important thing is to begin and take the first steps, trusting in God. What can't be done all at once can be done little by little. Much later, with hindsight, she often realized how impetuously she had proceeded. But at the time, with the absorption God gave her in the work, she didn't think of the difficulties.

We never know the ramifications of our first little steps. Teresa simply began by determining to live her own religious life with integrity. This led to the successful founding of her first monastery in Avila. Her inspired beginning led to the foundation of sixteen monasteries in her lifetime — fourteen she personally founded, two directed at a distance. All of these communities still exist today, four hundred years later — some living in the original sixteenth-century houses. Since Teresa's death, the number has grown to over eight hundred worldwide.

She also did something even more remarkable than founding her communities of women — she instituted her way of life among the Carmelite friars, playing a crucial role in finding the first men for the task and making the initial foundations at Duruelo (1568) and Pastrana (1569).

Leaving the Comfort Zone

Daring the dream means forgoing our personal safety. We must be willing to leave the familiarity and security of our comfort zone and move painfully into the holy insecurity of unknown and perhaps dangerous territory. Teresa faced a painful challenge when she left the Incarnation convent where she was satisfied on a certain level. She liked the convent and the cell where she lived. It was no easier for Teresa than it is for us to upset the status quo, disturb our calm, and leap into the fire of a brand new endeavor.

Making our dream come true means building support around us — and being willing to go it alone. It means persuading others to rally to the cause — and being willing to suffer gossip, criticism, and ridicule, sometimes to the point of severe opposition and slander. One of our greatest trials is being misunderstood by those we most want to understand us. As Teresa said, our friends are often the ones "who take the largest and most painful bite" out of us. For the foundation in Avila, Teresa had the support of those few sisters in her cell and her "lady companion," Doña Guiomar de Ulloa, who eventually provided a large part of the income. Guiomar helped rally the most learned man in Avila, and together they wrote to Rome to negotiate special papal permissions.

But there was a tremendous outcry at the Incarnation convent where the nuns felt insulted and wanted to throw Teresa into the prison cell for disobedience (yes, they had monastic "prisons"). No one in Avila would listen to her, calling the project a "whim," "the foolishness of women," and a "lot of nonsense." The uproar among the townspeople was vehement. A major issue was money. Since St. Joseph's was founded without an endowment, the nuns needed the alms of Avila for support. The mayor and the city council called a special meeting and unanimously declared that the convent would bring "notable harm to the republic" and furiously demanded its suppression.

For six months Teresa remained silent, not becoming involved or even speaking of the matter, which illustrates another stage in the realization of our dreams: the postponement, the waiting, the gestation period. Knowing when to wait is as integral to the dream as knowing when to act.

Teresa paid a high price to make her dreams come true — financial insecurity, inadequate housing and help, poor health, and arduous journeys involving "fleas, hobgoblins, and bad roads," as she joked with her traveling companion, Antonio Gaytán. Her journeys by mule or covered wagon were dangerous and difficult — but make for some of her best stories. "And oh! The inns!" she gasped. Lodging was often the most horrendous part of any trip. Teresa describes one in particular that was so dreadful, her little company left early, even though Teresa was seriously ill with a high fever. She said it was easier to suffer out in the open fields than in that miserable little room. As a result, she described this earthly life as a "night in a bad inn."

Her many mishaps on the road also added spice to the stories of her foundations. At the dedication of the Seville monastery, revelers shot artillery and hurled firecrackers. Some powder caught fire and a huge flame leaped up and blackened the stone arches of the cloister. It was fortunate no one was killed, Teresa says, and in the very next breath, observes that the red and yellow taffeta hangings were not damaged!

In Medina del Campo, Teresa's brave little band arrived at midnight and went to their house on foot to protect their secrecy. It was by the mercy of God that they were not mauled by any of the bulls being corralled at that hour for the next day's run.

In Salamanca, a university town, Teresa and María del Sacramento took over a large and filthy house previously occupied by students who were angry about leaving. María could not stop thinking about them and convinced herself that a student had hidden himself in one of the many garrets. The two women locked themselves into a room the first night — but ended up "spooking" themselves about dead bodies.

Hard Work and Business

No dream comes true without hard work. As Teresa often repeated: We must translate our dreams into deeds, our words
into works, our aspirations into action. When there was work
to be done, Teresa enjoyed being the first — cleaning, cooking,
even hammering in a nail. She sewed the first habit for Mariano and his companion when they joined her Reform, prepared
a special meal for the ascetic Peter of Alcántara to thank him
for all his help, and wouldn't let her tired and trusty messenger
leave Seville until she had cooked him an egg herself. She personally supervised much of the construction and repair work on
her buildings, wearing herself out "going about with the work-
men." In Salamanca she was so distraught over the construction
she wrote: "I said to the Lord, almost complaining, that either
He not order me to get involved in repair works or He help me
in this need." Teresa caused quite a commotion in Toledo when
she was dissatisfied with the small room set aside for the new
chapel. Seeking more space, she pounded her way through a
thin partition wall, terrifying a group of women sleeping on the
other side! Then with her characteristic tact and charm, Teresa
persuaded these lodgers to give up their bedroom to make the
chapel.

But the bulk of Teresa's work was administration — inevitable in the daring of any dream, however spiritual. "Although I
used to detest money and business matters," she wrote Lorenzo,
"it is the Lord's pleasure that I should engage in nothing else,
and that is no light cross. May His majesty grant me to serve
Him in this, for everything will pass away."

Teresa was not naive about money. She needed it: for the
purchase of land and houses; for construction and repairs; for
repaying debts and fighting lawsuits; for travel, food, clothing,
doctors, and medicines. "Wherever I am, so many expenses crop
up, if only for the porterage of letters," she told her brother. "It
worries me that things should cost so much." When María de
San José needed funds, Teresa wrote her: "I was very much attracted by the chance of getting some money which you could

have whenever you wanted it, for I do not want you to touch Beatriz's mother's money or Pablo's, as that must be used to pay off the principal, and if you start frittering it away on other things you will be left with a heavy burden of debt, which is really a terrible thing; so I should like to get you some help from here." Vexed by the demands of the canons of the Segovia cathedral, she said to María Bautista: "These Canons make me tired. They are asking now for an authorization from the Superior to force us to pay the ground-rent. If my Father has power to give this, it must be done in writing and through a lawyer, who will have to examine the license that he holds. If he has such a thing, for pity's sake let him send it to me soon, unless he would have me rotting in my grave first. If it were not for those miserable three thousand *maravedis*, we should be in the house by now."

Teresa's administrative burdens escalated tremendously over the years. "I have had so many letters during the last two days that they have driven me crazy," she wrote from Toledo. She had all she could handle "on site" in one foundation, yet at the same time repeatedly had to arrange for another one elsewhere. In a state of exhaustion after finally completing construction in Toledo, she could not diplomatically refuse the invitation of the princess of Eboli to travel immediately to Pastrana. While in Salamanca, a messenger arrived from Beas and turned her attention there. Teresa was beset with so many difficulties "on the road," even though each successive trial was as bad as the former one, and sometimes worse, she felt that the very change from one struggle to the next actually brought her relief. "Do you suppose," she wrote Gracián, when he was complaining about his responsibilities, "I have put up with only a few things I have not liked? No: I have endured a great many; and there are things that have to be endured if we are to meet a need."

When we dare our dream, we must be ready to make personal sacrifices and suffer many kinds of trials — including confusion, doubt, and the temptation to give up. This often afflicted Teresa. She regularly says, "I didn't know what to do." When St. Joseph's in Avila was finally dedicated in 1562, Teresa was intensely happy. But the glory lasted only three hours. Then a tremendous spiritual battle erupted in her, and she lost courage. She suffered a thousand doubts about whether she had done the right thing. Could she live up to her ideals? Could she be happy? Would she despair? She found herself in such darkness that she felt "like someone in the death agony." Yet only three hours earlier she'd been in seventh heaven. This led her to a profound meditation on the ephemeral nature of any earthly triumph. "There is no security in this life," she moaned. On the first night in Medina del Campo, Teresa suffered severe depression again over whether or not she had made the right decisions. This lack of confidence jeopardized the entire future of her work. Seven years later in Seville, despite her vast experience, she admitted that she didn't recognize herself: "I never felt more pusillanimous or cowardly in my life."

Sometimes it seemed that everything was failing in Avila. The city council sent an official denunciation of St. Joseph's to the royal council. A long lawsuit began — the first of many in Teresa's life — and negotiations required enormous effort on her part and the part of her friends. One of Teresa's greatest afflictions at this time — and throughout her life — was the suffering she brought upon others who supported her. She was heroically ready to undergo any trials alone, but very uneasy subjecting anyone else to persecution. But Teresa's friends were so fervent, they all considered the matter a part of them.

When we are weary, worn out by negotiations, threatened with lawsuits, filled with doubt and confusion, ready to compromise, we must not waver. We must remember the dream in all its pristine vigor, for we are doomed if we forget. We must move into a deeper level of trust in God, who can help us sustain our dream and also give us the determination to fulfill it.

Teresa had insufficient funding to create her first convent. But she trusted in God and proceeded, and then her brother Lorenzo's gold arrived from Ecuador. She did not want to say yes to the command of the princess of Eboli, but responded with trust in God's command. As a result, two new men joined her Reform. In Toledo, her companions laughed when she trusted the poor and ill-dressed student Andrada because his offer to help had a "mystery" about it. But in only two days he located a house for her when more respectable wealthy friends had found nothing in three months.

Trust in God is not blind trust. It does not mean sitting back and lazily doing nothing while we wait for God's miracles. Trust in God means acting in whatever way we can ourselves, and then trusting that our efforts will bear fruit — not according to our own limited expectations, but according to God's plan and providence. Teresa had to risk her first foundation before Lorenzo's gold arrived. She had to risk the journey to Pastrana in the princess of Eboli's elegant carriage, despite her incredible fatigue and reluctance. And she had to trust Andrada despite his ragamuffin appearance.

The Dying of the Dream

The dream of Teresa's foundations unfolds with heroism and humor, pathos and pain, mistakes and eventual triumph. Teresa's most vigorous persecutors in Avila eventually became the biggest supporters of St. Joseph's. By 1575, over a dozen new monasteries were initiated. Noblemen, bishops, and townships vied with one another to convince Teresa to found yet another. She was often hailed as a saint and mobbed when she visited a city.

And then the climate changed. Teresa entered that excruciating stage we all must confront: the dying of the dream. The reform she had struggled fifteen years to inaugurate now encountered such severe opposition, it was about to perish. Teresa was called a "restless gadabout," was "exiled" to a Castilian monastery of her choosing, and was forbidden to make any more foundations. Her nuns were put under the jurisdiction of the unreformed Calced Carmelites. Her friars were stripped of their authority and forced into silence. St. John of the Cross was kidnapped and imprisoned in Toledo. A malicious defamation campaign began against Teresa, Gracián, and other key figures. The persecution of the Teresian Reform is a tale of political intrigue, sexual innuendo, jealousy, pride, the messy mixture of church and state, the machinations of scoundrels, and the skillful maneuvering of a saint. The complex details are beyond the scope of this volume. It is important for us, however, to learn from Teresa's example. How do we cope in the face of opposition? How do we hold fast? How do we fight against the dying of the dream? We all need a breath of Teresa's warrior spirit.

"Nowadays, we are living, as it were, in war-time," Teresa wrote to María de San José, "and we must act with the greatest caution." During the three years of intense persecution from 1576 until 1579, Teresa never relaxed her warrior vigilance. "Let me know what foundation there is for this story about the nun who was supposed to be a virgin and had borne a child," she wrote to Gracián. "It seems to me the height of stupidity to invent an accusation like that." Because sexual slanders could be the most damaging, and Gracián lacked shrewdness and political sense, she had to advise him to stay away from the house of a loose-living woman he was ingenuously helping, for fear his enemies would accuse him of fathering her child. "I do not believe anything she says at all: she is a thorough fraud — God forgive me!" Teresa told him. "What a malicious person I am! But we have to be prepared for anything in this life.... Be on your guard, for I fear there will be greater publicity yet."

From her unofficial "imprisonment" — one year in Toledo and two in Avila — Teresa shrewdly devised a number of wartime strategies. She used a special trustworthy courier for her correspondence. "Always acknowledge the receipt of the letters I send you," she warned him. "I get worried about them, and with good reason. Remember it is most important to deliver all these letters secretly." Gracián's letters to her had to be addressed in María de San José's handwriting and then destroyed. "I must warn you, my Father," she wrote him. "This is a very risky matter. Tear up this letter at once." To maintain secrecy, Teresa created a series of pseudonyms, for fear the letters would be intercepted and fall into the wrong hands. She called herself "Laurencia" or "Angela," and she referred to Gracián as "Paul" or "Eliseo." The Calced friars were "owls" or "cats," the Discalced friars "eagles," and the nuns "doves" or "butterflies." In a magnificent piece of Teresian irony, the Inquisitors were "angels" and the Grand Inquisitor the "Arch-angel"! Christ himself became "Joseph," and the devil was referred to with a Spanish term roughly translated as "Hoofy."

Teresa's primary strategy was letter-writing — to mobilize support from her influential friends in key positions at crucial moments. Mariano was to talk to the king. Gracián was to give a present to the papal nuncio and write to his friends at the court in Madrid. Two friars were to go to Rome and approach the Carmelite general or the pope. "I can tell you I am suffering agonies at not being free to do what I am telling other people to do," Teresa complained. Sometimes she was frightened. "Oh, Jesus, how dreadful it is to be so far away when all these things are going on!" she wrote Gracián. "I assure you it is a heavy cross for me."

And yet Teresa's predominant response was peaceful and calm. "Oh, God help me, how free this woman feels amid all that is happening!" she wrote in 1576. "When things seem to be going best, I am generally less happy about them than I am now," she wrote the following year. And in the third and worst year of the opposition, she said: "All of a sudden our trials have become as bad as they can possibly be.... I am not greatly troubled about it." How could Teresa feel this way?

She knew that no matter how hard we work — with or without royal or papal support, a keen business sense, proper financing, and shrewd strategy — another crucial element helps our dream come true, an element of mystery and grace that is completely beyond the human mode. From the example of Teresa's life, we see that the powerful hand of God accomplishes all great works — provided we cooperate. We must trust in the "Lord of the house," for "He is wise, He is mighty, He understands what is suitable." With characteristic bite, Teresa chides us for wanting things to go our own way, according to our own time frame: "This is not a matter of your choosing but of the Lord's.... [I]t would be a nice kind of humility for you to want to choose for yourselves!" All the odds were against Teresa at the time of the persecution. Her friars weakened and didn't know what to do. Her friends disappeared or faltered. The king was silent for months. But she trusted in God's revelation to her years before, during a period of great anxiety: "Do what lies in your power; surrender yourself to me, and do not be disturbed about anything." So she suffered her confinement, concocted plans, and continued writing letter after letter. As a result, an independent Discalced province finally emerged, and her beloved Gracián became the first provincial.

Teresa's ultimate strategy, for times of peace as well as war, is summed up in a sentence from the *Soliloquies:* "Let us try hard, let us trust hard." If we bring our holy audacity and humble determination to God, who is the giver of every dream, then God will do the rest to make our dream come true.

Meditation

In the following texts, Teresa describes the courage and determination we need to take risks and dare our impossible dream. She shares her own difficulties over leaving the comfort zone and entering the battle of heroic endeavor, often completely alone. Her own anguish and doubt are expressed so universally, we see ourselves in her temptation to give up and look for rest.

Then we meet Teresa, the shrewd businesswoman, buying a house in Burgos with her friend Dr. Aguiar. Some of her most entertaining stories come from these days on the road, making her many foundations. We hear about getting lost on the journey to the first friars' monastery in Duruelo, spooking herself over the thought of dead bodies in Salamanca, and the scorching trip to Seville when the ropes from the barge crossing the Guadalquivir broke and her wagon floated down the river.

What was Teresa's response to her misadventures? She explains how she tried to ignore her distaste for these trials, her strong aversion to traveling, and her dismay over bad weather and poor health. This leads to her determination to suffer any hardship to fulfill the will of God and make his dream her own.

The letters written to Gracián at the height of opposition to the Reform show the broad range of Teresa's capacities as a leader and feelings as a woman. We see her anguish over Rubeo's death and her political shrewdness in dealing with the king, the nuncio, and the two friars en route to Rome and in giving the same answers under interrogation. Her motherly concern for Gracián's safety is juxtaposed with her distress and disillusionment with him for not having acted on her advice sooner. Above all, we see her absolute trust in God's guidance, even though all seems lost.

In the final texts given in the following section, which are taken from various stages in Teresa's life, she gives God the credit for giving her the dream and keeping it alive at all cost.

Teresian Texts: Dare the Dream

O greatness of God! How You manifest Your power in giving courage to an ant! How true, my Lord, that it is not because of You that those who love You fail to do great works but because of our own cowardice and pusillanimity. Since we are never determined, but full of human prudence and a thousand fears, You, consequently, my God, do not do your marvelous and great works. Who is more fond than You of giving, or of serving even at a cost to Yourself, when there is someone open to receive? May it please Your Majesty that I render You some service and that I not have to render an accounting for all that I have received.

(*F* 2.7)

By what you do in deed — that which you can — His Majesty will understand that you would do much more.... We shouldn't build castles in the air. The Lord doesn't look so much at the greatness of our works as at the love with which they are done.

And if we do what we can, His Majesty will enable us each day to do more and more, provided that we do not quickly tire. But during the little while this life lasts — and perhaps it will last a shorter time than each one thinks — let us offer the Lord interiorly and exteriorly the sacrifice we can. His Majesty will join it with that which He offered on the cross to the Father for us. Thus even though our works are small they will have the value our love for Him would have merited had they been great.

(IC 7.4.14–15)

What we were doing seemed absurd to everyone. Afterward I saw that they were more than right. For when the Lord is pleased that I found one of these houses, it seems that until after the foundation is made my mind doesn't admit any reason that would seem sufficient to set the work aside. After the deed is done, all the difficulties come before me together.

(F 3.4)

I often thought that the riches God placed in [me] were meant for some great purpose. What was later to come about never passed through my mind, because it didn't seem then to be something possible. There was no basis for even being able to imagine it, although my desires to be of some help to some soul as time went on had grown much greater. And I often felt like one who has a great treasure stored up and desires that all enjoy it, but whose hands are bound and unable to distribute it. So it seemed my soul was bound because the favors the Lord was granting it during those years were very great, and I thought that I was not putting them to good use.

(F 1.6)

Well then, being consoled in having the permissions, my concern grew in that there was no friar in the province that I knew of who could begin this work, nor any layman who desired to make such a start. I didn't do anything but beg our Lord that he would awaken at least one person. Neither did I have a house or the means to get one. Here I was, a poor discalced nun, with-out help from anywhere — only from the Lord — weighed down with patent letters and good desires, and without there being any possibility of my getting the work started. Neither courage nor hope failed, for since the Lord had given the one thing, He would give the other. Everything now seemed very possi-ble, and so I set to work.

(*F* 2.6)

❖

I felt the severest pain because on the one hand the terrible dis-turbances and trials the new monastery would cost were partly represented to me, and on the other hand I was very happy in my own monastery. Although I had been discussing it before, I hadn't done so with as much determination or certitude as was necessary to bring it about. These words seemed to compel me, and since I saw I would be starting something that would disturb my calm I was doubtful about what to do.

(*L* 32.12)

I had been consoled and at peace there and had found time for many hours of prayer. I saw I was about to place myself in a fire, for the Lord had already told me I was going to undergo a great cross, although I never thought it would be as great as I afterward found out it was. Nonetheless, I was happy in going; and since the Lord had desired me to go, I was disturbed that I hadn't entered the battle immediately.

(*L* 35.10)

When our intention became known in the city, there was much criticism. Some were saying I was crazy; others were hoping for an end to that nonsense. To the bishop — according to what he told me later — the idea seemed very foolish. But he didn't then let me know this; neither did he hinder me, for he loved me much and didn't want to hurt me. My friends said a great deal against the project. But I didn't pay much attention to them. For that which to them seemed doubtful, to me seemed so easy that I couldn't persuade myself that it would fail to be a true success.

(F 3.3)

I saw clearly the toil it would bring upon me since I was very much alone and had hardly any means.... In procuring the money, acquiring the house, signing the contract for it, and fixing it up, I went through so many trials of so many kinds that now I'm amazed I was able to suffer them. In some of them I was completely alone; although my companion did what she could. But she could do little, and so little that it almost amounted to nothing more than to have everything done in her name and as her gift and all the rest of the trouble was mine. Sometimes in distress I said: "My Lord, how is it You command things that seem impossible? For if I were at least free, even though I am a woman! But bound on so many sides, without the money or the means to raise it or to obtain the brief or anything, what can I do, Lord?"

(L 33.11)

✤

There were doubts as to whether those who lived here would be happy with so much austerity. What if they lacked food? Wasn't it all foolishness? Who got me involved in all this since I already had a monastery to live in? All that the Lord had commanded me, and the great deal of advice, and the prayers that for more than two years had gone on almost without cease, all was erased from my memory as though it had never been.... The devil raised doubts in me also about how I wanted to shut myself up in so austere a house, and with my many illnesses. How would I be able to endure so much penance and leave a monastery that was large and pleasant and where I had always been so happy? And how could I leave so many friends, for perhaps those in the new house would not be to my liking? I had obligated myself to a great deal; perhaps I would despair.

(L 36.7–8)

To this anguish were joined all the difficulties that those who had strongly criticized the project could bring up. I understood clearly that those persons were right. It seemed impossible for me to go ahead with what had been begun. Just as previously everything seemed easy to me when I reflected that I was doing it for God, so now my temptation constricted the Lord's power to such an extent that it didn't seem I had received any favor from Him. Only my lowliness and powerlessness did I have before me. Well now, supported by something so miserable, what success could I hope for? Had I been alone, I think I could have suffered their situation. But to think that my companions, after the opposition with which they had left, had to return to their houses was a painful thing to bear. Also, it seemed to me that since this first attempt had gone wrong, everything that I had understood I must do for the Lord in the future would not come about.... With all this anguish that kept me truly depressed, I didn't let my companions know anything because I didn't want to cause them more distress than they already had.

(F 3.11–12)

The Lord did not let His poor servant suffer long, for never did He fail to succor me in my tribulations.... I began to recall my strong resolutions to serve the Lord and my desires to suffer for Him. I reflected that if I were to fulfill these desires I couldn't go about seeking rest.... I had nothing to fear, for since I desired trials, these troubles were good; that the greater the opposition the greater the gain. And why did I lack courage to serve one whom I owed so much?

(L 36.9)

✤

From the vigil of St. Matthias, when we began living in the hospital, until the vigil of St. Joseph we were conferring about this and that house. There were so many obstacles that we could not buy any of those that were for sale....

I then remembered the one I mentioned that we had disregarded. I thought, even though it's as bad as they say we can take care of our present need and later on sell it....

It was arranged that I go to see it. It pleased me to such an extreme that if they had asked for twice as much as they did, it would have seemed cheap to me. I am not exaggerating, because two years before they were offering the owner that much, and he did not want to sell it. The next day a priest and Doctor Aguiar went there, and when the latter learned of the amount of money that would be acceptable, he wanted to sign the contract at once. I had informed some of my friends, and they had told me that if I gave this amount I was giving five hundred ducats too much. I told Doctor Aguiar, but he thought the price was cheap if I gave what was asked for. I was of the same mind....

No one thought the house would be sold for so little. Thus, as the news spread, the buyers began to appear and say that the priest who sold it gave it away practically and that the sale should be nullified because of the great fraud. The good priest suffered very much....

As soon as I saw it and how everything was as though made to order for us and done so quickly, it seemed like a dream. By bringing us to such a paradise, our Lord repaid us generously for what we had suffered. Because of the garden, the view, and the water, the property is nothing else but that. May He be blessed forever, amen....

In drawing up the contracts there was no little trouble, because one minute they were satisfied with the guarantors, the next minute they wanted the money; and they made many other vexing demands....

(F 31.32–42)

Although we left in the morning, we got lost because we didn't know the road; and since the place [Duruelo] is little known, we couldn't get much information about where it was. Thus, our traveling that day was very trying and the sun was very hot. When we thought we were near, we discovered we had just as far to go. I always remember the tiredness we felt and the

wrong roads we took on that journey. The result was that we
arrived shortly before nightfall.

When we entered the house it was in such a state that we
dared not remain there that night; it wasn't at all clean and was
filled with vermin. It had a fairly good entrance way, a room
double in size, a loft, and a small kitchen. This was all we had
for our monastery. I figured that the entrance way could serve
as the chapel, the loft as the choir, which would adapt well, and
the room for sleeping.

My companion, although much better than I and very fond
of penance, couldn't bear the thought of my planning to found
a monastery there and said to me: "Surely, Mother, there isn't
a soul, however good, that could put up with this. Don't even
consider it."

(*F* 13.3)

Once my companion was locked in that room, it seems she
calmed down a little with regard to the students, although she
didn't do anything but look about from side to side, still fearful. And the devil must have helped by bringing to her mind
thoughts about the danger. Her thoughts then began to disturb
me, for with my weak heart, not much was needed. I asked her
why she was looking around since no one could get in there.
She answered: "Mother, I was wondering what would happen
if I were to die now; what would you do here all alone?" If that
had happened it would have been a hard thing for me to take.
And I began to think a little about it and even become afraid.
Because as for dead bodies, although I am not afraid of them,
my heart gets weak even when I'm not alone. And since the
tolling of the bells helped matters along, for, as I said, it was
the vigil of All Souls, the devil had a good means of making
us squander our thoughts on trifles. When he sees that one
has no fear of him, he looks for other devices. I said to her:
"Sister, when this happens, I'll think about what to do; now, let
me sleep." Since we had just spent two bad nights, sleep came
soon and took away our fears.

(*F* 19.5)

Although we hurried along on our journey, we did not reach
Seville until the Thursday before Trinity Sunday, after having endured scorching heat. Even though we did not travel during
siesta time, I tell you, Sisters, that since the sun was beating
on the wagons, getting into them was like stepping into purga-
tory. Sometimes by thinking of hell, at other times by thinking
that something was being done and suffered for God, those Sisters journeyed with much happiness and joy. The six souls who
were with me were of the kind that made me think I was daring enough to go off with them to the land of the Turks and that
they had the fortitude, or better, our Lord gave them the fortitude, to suffer for Him; for this was the subject of their desires
and conversations....

Something else happened to us which got us into a tight
spot while we were crossing the Guadalquivir on a barge.
When it was time for the wagon to cross, it was not possible to make a straight crossing where the rope was, but they
had to wind their way across; the rope from the other shore
was of some help by flowing with the barge. However, it happened that those who were holding the rope let it go, or I don't
know what happened, for the barge went off with the wagon
and without rope or oars. I felt much more concern in seeing
the anxiety of the boatman than I did about the danger. We
were all praying; the others were all screaming.

A gentleman watching us from a nearby castle was moved
with pity and sent someone to help, for the barge then had
not yet broken loose and our brothers were pulling, using all
their strength; but the force of the water dragged them along
to the point that some fell to the ground. Indeed, the boatman's son caused in me feelings of great devotion, which I
never forget — he must have been ten or eleven years old —
for the way he was working so hard upon seeing his father
in this difficulty made me praise our Lord. But as His Majesty
always gives trials in a compassionate way, so He did here. It
happened that the boat got stuck on part of a sand bar where
there was not much water; thus a rescue was made possible.
Since nightfall had come, we would not have known how to

continue our journey if someone from the castle had not come to guide us.

I had not thought of dealing with these things because they are of little importance, and I could have mentioned many bad incidents that occurred on our journeys. But I have been urged to enlarge on my account of this trip.

(*F* 24.6, 10–11)

✢

Although my human nature sometimes finds these trials distasteful, my determination to suffer for this great God does not lessen. Thus I told Him not to pay any attention to my feelings of weakness when He orders me to do what would please Him, for with His help I would not fail to do it. There was cold weather and snow at the time. That which daunted me most was my lack of health, for when I have my health everything seems easy to me.

(*F* 31.12)

But I saw clearly that our Lord was giving me strength. It happened to me at times when a foundation was being planned that I would be so sick and have so many pains that I would get very anxious. It seemed to me that I wasn't even able to remain in my cell without lying down. I would turn to our Lord, complain to His Majesty, and ask how He desired me to do what I couldn't. Afterward, although I still felt the hardship, His Majesty gave me strength, and with the fervor and solicitude he gave, it seems I forgot about myself.... From what I now remember, fear of the hardship involved never prevented me from making a foundation even though I felt strong aversion to the traveling, especially the long journeys. But once we got started, the journey seemed easy to me, and I considered for whose service it was made and reflected that in that house the Lord would be praised.

(*F* 18.4–5)

God was pleased to . . . give me such health that it seemed to me I had never been sick. I was surprised and reflected on how very important it is not to consider our weak state of health or any opposition that occurs when we understand that something serves the Lord since God is powerful enough to make the weak strong and the sick healthy. And when our Lord does not do this, suffering will be the best thing for our souls; and fixing our eyes on His honor and glory, we should forget ourselves. What is the purpose of life and health save that they be lost for so great a King and Lord?

(*F* 28.18)

❖

I am afraid letters are being intercepted, so I am writing to tell you what is happening. In case your Paternity has not gone where you said you were going I am sending another messenger to Valladolid, to let the Mother Prioress know how she is to answer, for Roque lays great stress on our not making different replies — it would be the end of everything for us if we did. He sends me a copy of what he has sent her. I have already instructed the other persons concerned. Please God it may not be necessary, for it is a great shame to see these souls subject to people who cannot understand them.

Still, it is only about my Paul that I am anxious and troubled. If only I could see him free! Really, I don't know why, but I can't feel troubled about anything else, even if I want to. The Lord will provide, and if you are always on your guard in these parts, I shall be satisfied so long as you don't go yonder. But I have sore misgivings, for even in the bare coming and going necessary for saying Mass there cannot fail to be danger.

I am amazed at the turn things are taking, and I should be glad to know you had left the place where you are now and gone to some place where we could be sure about you. For pity's sake, keep me informed of your whereabouts, or I shall be distracted when I want to send you any information. . . .

There are only two reasons why I want you to go. One is my great fear that they will seize you where you are now, and if that is possible — God save you from it! — it would be better for you to get away. The other is that we should see what line the Nuncio is going to adopt towards you before you go to the King. In any case it will be advisable for you to have an interview (with the Nuncio)....

O what precious treasures are these, my Father! No price will purchase them, since through them may be gained so worthy a crown. When I remember that Our Lord Himself and all His saints travelled by this road, I can only envy your Paternity, as I no longer deserve to suffer, but only to know how one so dear to me is suffering, which is a far sorer trial.

To-morrow we shall arrange for Julián de Avila to go to Madrid one day soon to make an act of allegiance to the Nuncio as our superior, and try to get into his good graces, and beg him not to give us over to the Calced. Meanwhile, I shall write to several people to see if they can make him more kindly disposed to your Paternity....

May the Lord give us His help, for they cannot make us offend Him; and I have the saintly Paul with me and no one can make me break my promise to that saint....

We have no cause for fear, my Father: we must praise God, Who is leading us by the way He Himself walked.

(Le 239 to Gracián)

I was intensely grieved at the news which I received about our Father General. I feel deeply moved by it. On the day I heard it I wept and wept — I could do nothing else — and I felt very much distressed at all the trouble we have caused him, which he certainly did not deserve: if we had gone to him about the matter everything would have been smoothed out. God forgive the person who has continually put obstacles in the way; for, though you had little confidence in my suggestion, I could have come to an understanding with your Paternity. The Lord will bring it all right; but I am sorry about the things I have described, and also about your Paternity's sufferings, for really to read what you wrote me in your first letter — I have had two from you since your interview with the Nuncio — was as bitter a draught as death.

I must tell you, my Father, I was dreadfully upset at your not having shown him those papers at once: you must have been advised by someone who cares little for your Paternity's sufferings. I am very glad to think you will now have learned by experience to guide your affairs along the road which they will have to take, instead of going against the current, which I have always warned you about. There have really been obstacles in our way the whole time, so we must say no more about it, for God orders things so that His servants may suffer. . . .

We are all agreed here that our friars must not go to Rome, especially now that our Father General is dead, for these reasons. First, it cannot be done secretly; the Calced friars may seize them before they leave here and that would be as good as putting them to death. Secondly, in that case, they will lose both the documents and the money. Thirdly, they have no experience of negotiations at Rome. Fourthly, when they get there, now that our Father General has gone, they will be arrested as if they were fugitives, for after all, as I have been saying to Father Mariano, they will be wandering through the streets with no one to come to their aid. If with all the influence at our disposal here we could do nothing for Fray John [of the Cross], what could we possibly do (for them) there?

(*Le* 253 to Gracián)

❖

Oh, God help me, how many obstacles I have seen in these business matters that seemed impossible to overcome, and how easy it was for His Majesty to remove them. . . . [I]n these foundations we creatures have done next to nothing. The Lord has directed all by means of such low beginnings that only His Majesty could have raised the work to what it now is. May he always be blessed, amen.

(*F* 13.7)

You will see that in part these houses, most of them, have not been founded by men but by the powerful hand of God and that His Majesty is very fond of advancing the works He accomplishes provided we cooperate. From where do you think a useless woman like me, subject to obedience, without even a *maravedi* [a monetary denomination], with no one to help me in any way, could get the power for such great works? ... Well, it could not be because I am from the nobility that He has given me such honor. In whatever way you want to look at this you will recognize that it is His work.

(F 27.11–12)

He enlightens me thus in anything I manage to do well, for each day I am more amazed at the little talent I have for anything. And don't think that what I'm saying comes from humility, for each day I see it more clearly. It seems our Lord desires me and all others to know that it is only His Majesty who does these works.... I would like to praise our Lord again for it. But even for this I'm no good, nor do I know how He puts up with me.

(F 29.24)

The safest way is to want only what God wants. He knows more than we ourselves do, and He loves us. Let us place ourselves in His hands so that His will may be done in us, and we cannot err if with a determined will we always maintain this attitude.

(IC 6.9.16)

Chapter 5

The Mystery of Suffering

What a tremendous good it is to suffer trials and persecutions for Him. For the increase of the love of God I saw in my soul and many other things reached such a point that I was amazed; and this makes me unable to stop desiring trials.

(L 33.4)

Suffering is a mysterious and inescapable part of life. It afflicts us from the outside and from deep within our own souls. We suffer at the hands of others — those we love as well as those we do not — and seemingly even from the hands of God. We suffer from illness, fatigue, and emotional upheavals, from worry, anxiety, and misunderstanding. When we read St. Teresa, we discover a life of enormous suffering. Teresa allowed suffering to ravage her so deeply, she eventually broke through into that exquisite experience of ravishment. She often begins speaking painfully and fearfully, feeling disturbed and troubled, battling her own thoughts, and unable to recollect herself. But then she ends up in peaceful resolution: "How worthwhile this war and strife is!" Moving through Teresa's writings, we notice how often she voices the same laments: "I was afraid," "I didn't know what to do," "I thought he would make fun of me," "I did nothing but weep."

Physical Pain

Poor health is an arena for enormous human suffering. Teresa has much to teach us here because for over forty years, she never

111

spent a single day without physical pain. For most of her life she suffered such nausea that she vomited daily and couldn't eat until noon. She suffered the little illnesses that afflict us all — colds, headaches, stomachaches, toothaches, and flus. But she also suffered from high fevers, fainting spells, heart trouble, neuritis, tinnitus, her maimed left arm, a three-year paralysis, severe convulsions, a four-day coma, and the influenza that almost killed her in 1580, aged her terribly, and left her palsied for the last two years of her life. When she was examined in Burgos by Gracián's friend, Dr. Antonio Aguiar, he said no part of her body was sound. In a letter to Antonio Gaytán she said: "I was going to say I am well, because when I have nothing the matter beyond my usual ailments, that is good health for me."

As a result of her experience, Teresa teaches us that poor health is not an obstacle to spiritual growth but actually enhances it. Why? We learn patience and surrender. We learn how to transcend the body and rise above both sickness and health altogether. Preoccupation with good health is often due to laziness, pampering, and a desire for comfort. In a most amusing passage from *The Way of Perfection*, Teresa exposes the self-indulgence that keeps us from prayer: "We stay away one day because our head ached, another because it was just now aching, and three more so that it won't ache again!" She urges us not to complain about light illnesses that we can bear on our feet because we'll never stop lamenting. We must remember the poor and homeless who have no one to complain to.

Serious illness is another matter. Teresa was deathly ill often enough to know that there are times when we must come to terms with sickness. She describes how she prayed when bodily pains became intolerable for her and explains that health and bodily strength are not prerequisites for prayer.

"Worry over our health will not improve our health," Teresa wrote. "This I know. And I also know that the whole affair doesn't lie in what pertains to the body, for this is what is least important." Yet we have seen how Teresa paid attention to the body and recognized its legitimate needs. Like any good woman, she was interested in health remedies and frequently exchanged medicinal advice in her letters. For urinary complaints she recommended a morning dose of rose-hips, "picked when they are ripe and dry." For iron-deficiency anemia she recommended a mixture of sulphur-wort, coriander, powdered eggshells, oil, rosemary, and lavender. Nuts were good for "laxity of the stomach" and the scent of orange-flower water for the heart — "but it should not be drunk." And "whatever anyone says, be sure not to take sarsaparilla water," she repeated emphatically. If someone needed a purgative, she advocated a mighty syrup elegantly called the "King of Medes." Teresa also took fragrant South American resins called *caraña* and *anime* and made them into pastilles to throw into a brazier to purify the air and help colds and headaches.

At times Teresa asked for sickness; at other times she begged for healing. She considered this a mistake, since God alone knows best what is fitting for us. It disturbed her terribly that her physical weakness forced her to spend so much time taking care of herself. She frequently wept over it and then became so angry, she ended up hating herself. But through this as in all else, Teresa learned how to let go of her own will and trust in God. She vehemently asserts that we must "determine once and for all to swallow death and the lack of health," or there will be no hope for us.

Emotional Disturbances

Teresa uses the term "melancholy" throughout her writings to describe a broad series of mental and emotional sufferings that range from listlessness and chronic depression to low-grade panic attacks, nervous breakdowns, and insanity. Melancholy is such a serious problem, Teresa addresses it in depth and would mention it "another hundred times" if she could. The affliction is characterized by sullenness, withdrawal, and outbreaks of violent anger. Today we describe this same dysfunction in terms of depression, passive aggression, and possibly even PMS. The melancholy personality is negative and gloomy, prone to self-absorption, self-pity, and self-will, and extremely manipulative.

Teresa's analysis and treatment of melancholia rivals that of any modern therapist. Chapter 7 of the *Foundations* is an excellent little treatise on this affliction. Teresa teaches her prioresses how to handle melancholics in their convents. How can we use this vast experience to help us through our own bouts of depression and emotional disturbance? What coping strategies can be devised from Teresa's wisdom?

Teresa's emphasis on fear tactics and punishment is not without validity. We must be stopped from raging and raising a ruckus. Since we are out of control, we need to be restrained. According to Teresa, one day or as long as a month in a prison cell may not be too extreme! This mental or emotional suffering is a sickness, a danger to the soul, and a martyrdom. We must not allow it to harm ourselves or others, hence the need for constraint.

Sometimes medications help. Teresa recommends meat to "ground" us — solid nutritional advice given today as well by the best macrobiotic experts on diet and stress. This is not a time for solitude but for keeping busy, so we "do not have the opportunity to be imagining things, for herein lies all the trouble." We should also pray only for short periods of time during these upheavals because prayer in this state becomes no more than self-absorption: We senselessly rehash things over and over, feeling more and more sorry for ourselves because of what "they" are doing to us. We must never excuse ourselves for our outrageous behaviors, no matter how tormented we feel. We obviously need understanding and compassion from those around us, but we must never abuse their goodness by manipulating it for our own purposes.

The Meaning of Suffering

Why do we suffer? Teresa is not superficial or glib. Her testimony is powerful because she suffered so intensely and yet grew more luminous and integrated. She sometimes complained to God for allowing her to suffer so many torments. But as a mystic, that is, immersed in the Mystery, she discovered both meaning and value in suffering.

In itself, suffering has no value and can even embitter us. But when we suffer in union with the crucified Christ, we become more human and holy. Suffering is a dreadful teacher but often the beginning of the best in us. Suffering and creativity are often interdependent. Pain produces a terrible tension released in our creative response. Suffering can be like a grain of sand in an oyster: It can create a magnificent pearl.

In some profound way, suffering makes us "ready" for God by hollowing us out and increasing our capacity for the divine. Those who experience God deeply are those who have been prepared by trials. Suffering places us in a crucible, and like gold, we emerge refined, purified, and strengthened. "Afterward these trials that seemed unbearable become small, and one wants to return to suffering if the Lord will be more served by it." Either we believe this or we don't, Teresa insists, and asks, if we do, then "Why do we kill ourselves?"

We suffer for love's sake — for love of God and one another. The measure for being able to suffer is love. Those who love more want to suffer more, in imitation of the laborious life Christ lived. If Christ suffers, we who love him also want to suffer with him.

The meaning of suffering is summed up in the mystery of the cross. Teresa believed that the cross is the gift God gives his intimate friends. "He wants to lead you as though you were strong, giving you the cross here below, something that His Majesty always had. What better friendship than that He desire for you what He desired for Himself?" When John of the Cross was imprisoned and tortured in Toledo, she wrote to Gracián: "God's treatment of His friends is terrible, though they have really nothing to complain of, as He did the same to His own Son."

Teresa wrote three poems describing the cross in ecstatic, positive, life-giving terms: "my life's delightful rest"; "my wel-

116 ± *The Mystery of Suffering*

come [and] protecting banner"; the "Tree of life," whose fruit "tastes like the God of paradise." The cross is not merely a symbol of death — despite the horror of crucifixion — but also a symbol of life and resurrection. We must see the pain of it as growing pain or labor pain, resulting in the birth of new life.

Whenever we suffer, we speak of being given a cross that we are called to embrace. How can we use a tender word like "embrace" for the terror of the cross? Because in some paradoxical way, we are called to love the cross. If we do not embrace our cross but merely "drag it along," it hurts and wearies us and breaks us to pieces. "However, if the cross is loved, it is easy to bear; this is certain." Teresa does not say this lightly, but out of a lifetime of blood and vomit, loneliness and exhaustion, pain and persecution. We cannot be reasonable about the cross God gives us in this life. God will give us the strength to bear it by blessing us not merely with water but also with the best inebriating wine.

Those who truly grow do not run from suffering but desire it. This is no easier for us than it was for Teresa, who desired trials, on the one hand, and refused them, on the other. We must take courage, for the sovereign hand of God will help us. Following the path to perfection is a much longer and more difficult martyrdom than being quickly beheaded! But we must not back down or turn away.

Teresa was eloquent about the meaning of suffering. But she was no masochist, wallowing in suffering for its own sake. She embraced suffering because she knew its reward. From the very first pages of the *Life* until she concludes the final pages of *The Interior Castle*, she frequently repeats one of her favorite themes: "The pay begins *now!*" She would not exchange all the suffering in her life for all the world's treasures. Nor should we, for when we least expect it, God gives us medicine and heals our wounds; calms the storm and floods the sky with sunlight; gives us the victory in battle; waters the garden; takes pity on the exhausted little bird who cannot find rest and places it in the nest. If we don't believe Teresa's testimony here, she says she's not going to break her head trying to convince us. We'll have to learn for ourselves.

Meditation

In the following texts, Teresa first describes the unbearable torments she suffered after her violent treatments at Becedas and her four-day coma; she then describes the after-effects, which lasted for years. After she movingly complains about the helplessness we feel in spirit when the body is weak or ill, she heroically calls us to stop lamenting and seeking rest or health.

Then Teresa describes what she does when her pain becomes intolerable and tells us how to pray when we are sick. She assures us that taking care of ourselves is both necessary and an expression of our love for God. In a letter to Lorenzo, written during one of her own sickly periods, she explains that she cannot pray and is trying to get well. Then she openly confesses irritation over her uselessness.

In the following section, Teresa describes the difficulties of coping with someone suffering an emotional upheaval. She gives María Bautista advice on how to respond to her own disturbance, largely by ignoring it. Her brother Pedro is a more serious case. In a frank letter to her brother Lorenzo, Teresa shows concern for Pedro but admits how hard she finds it to deal with him. Because Pedro is typically fussy and manipulative — classic signs of melancholy — Teresa gives Lorenzo practical advice on how to respond to his tactics.

The next stirring series of quotations challenges us not to escape suffering but to take up our cross and follow the crucified Christ, no matter how much we stumble and fall. The more contemplative we are, the greater our trials. The final group of texts shows us the tremendous reward awaiting us if we suffer gladly and bravely.

Teresa wrote the letter to her nuns in Seville (the very last text in what follows) at the height of their suffering, when María de San José was deposed as prioress, and the community was torn apart by dissension. Teresa envies them their troubles and gives sound advice for coping in times of trial. When we are struggling ourselves, we should read this letter over and over, as though Teresa were speaking directly to us with all her motherly love and concern.

Teresian Texts: The Mystery of Suffering

Only the Lord can know the unbearable torments I suffered within myself: my tongue, bitten to pieces; my throat unable to let even water pass down — from not having swallowed anything and from great weakness that oppressed me; everything seeming to be disjointed; the greatest confusion in my head; all shriveled and drawn together in a ball. The result of the torments of those four days is that I was unable to stir, not an arm or a foot, neither hand nor head, unable to move as though I was dead; only one finger on my right hand it seems I was able to move. Since there was no way of touching me, because I was so bruised that I couldn't endure it, they moved me about by a sheet, one of the nuns at one end and another at the other.

This lasted until Easter. My only relief was that if they did not touch me, the pains often stopped, and on account of this bit of rest, I considered myself really well; for I was fearful I would lose patience. And so I was very happy to be without such sharp and continuous pains, although the quartan fevers that remained with their accompanying severe chills were so harsh that I found them unbearable; the lack of appetite was very great.

(*L* 6.1)

Though I was cured of that very serious illness, I have always up till now had illnesses and still have some that are serious enough and of various sorts, although lately not so severe. In particular, for twenty years I had vomiting spells every morning so that I could not eat anything until afternoon; sometimes I had to wait longer. From the time I began to receive Communion more frequently, I have had to vomit at night before going to bed. And it is more painful because I have to induce it with a feather or some other thing, for if I let this go the sickness I feel becomes very bad. I am almost never, in my opinion, without many pains, and sometimes very severe ones, especially in the heart, although the sickness that gripped me almost continually occurs very seldom. I was cured eight years ago of the harsh paralysis and other illnesses with fever that I frequently suffered. All these illnesses now bother me so little that I am often glad, thinking the Lord is served by something.

(*L* 7.11)

Often I complain to our Lord about how much the poor soul shares in the illness of the body. It seems the soul can do nothing but abide by the laws of the body and all its needs and changes.

One of the great trials and miseries of life, I think, is this helplessness experienced when there is no strong spirit to bring the body into submission. For if the soul is alert, I don't consider the suffering of illness and pain a problem, even though they may be a trial, for the soul is praising God and accepting this as coming from His hand. But it is a terrible thing on the one hand to be suffering and on the other not to be doing anything. This is especially true if the soul has experienced great desires not to rest interiorly or exteriorly but to occupy itself completely in the service of its great God. It has no other remedy here than patience, knowledge of its misery, and abandonment of itself to the will of God who makes use of it for what He wants and in the way He wants.

(*F* 29.2-3)

Since I am so sickly, I have always been tied down without being worth anything until I determined to pay no attention to the body or to my health. Now what I do doesn't amount to much; but since God desired that I understand this trick of the devil, who put the thought in my head that I would lose my health, I said: What difference does it make if I die; or at the thought of rest, I answered: I no longer need rest but the cross; and so with other thoughts. I have seen clearly that on very many occasions, even though I am in fact very sickly, that it was a temptation from the devil or from my own laziness — for afterward when I wasn't so cared for and pampered, I had much better health.

(L 13.7)

With regard to some of the weaknesses and little illnesses of women, forget about complaining of them, for sometimes the devil makes us imagine these pains. They are things that come and go. If you do not lose the habit of speaking and complaining about everything — unless you do so to God — you will never finish your lamenting.... A fault this body has is that the more comfort we try to give it the more needs it discovers. It's amazing how much comfort it wants.

(W 11.2)

❖

When bodily pains and sickness become intolerable I have the custom of making interior acts of supplication to the Lord as best I can, that if His Majesty be served by my doing so He might give me patience and I might remain in this state until the end of the world. Well, since I was suffering so severely this time, I was helping myself through these acts and resolutions so as to be able to bear it.

(L 31.3)

Bodily strength is not necessary [for prayer] but only love and a habit; and the Lord always provides the opportunity if we desire. I say "always" because, although on occasion and also sometimes in sickness we are impeded from having hours free for solitude, there is no lack of other time when we have the health for this. And even in sickness itself and these other occasions the prayer is genuine when it comes from a soul that loves to offer the sickness up and accept what is happening and be conformed to it and to the other thousand things that happen. Prayer is an exercise of love, and it would be incorrect to think that if there is no time for solitude there is no prayer at all.

(L 7.12)

Sometimes I worry because I see I do so little in His service and that I must necessarily take time for a body as weak and wretched as mine, more than I would want. Once I was in prayer, and the hour for going to bed came; I was feeling many pains and had to induce the usual vomiting. Since I saw I was so bound to myself and that my spirit on the other hand wanted more time, I got so wearied I began to weep freely and grow distressed. (This has happened not only once but, as I say, often.) It seems to me I became angry with myself in such a way that I then truly hated myself. But usually I know I don't hold myself in abhorrence, nor do I fail to do what I see is necessary for myself. And may it please the Lord that I do not care for myself more than is necessary, as sometimes I'm afraid I do. This time of which I'm speaking, the Lord appeared to me and greatly comforted me and told me I should suffer and do these things for love of Him because they were now necessary for my life.

(*L* 40.20)

I think good will come out of this evil, for I am beginning to acquire the habit of using an amanuensis, which I might have done before for unimportant letters. I shall keep on doing it now. I have taken some pills and am a great deal better. I think starting to fast in Lent was bad for me: it was not only headache that I had, but heart trouble as well. The heart is much better now, and during the last two days the head has improved too, and it was that that tried me most — quite a lot, indeed. What I was really afraid of was that I might become completely helpless. It would have been very rash of me to try to pray, and Our Lord well knows what harm it would have done me, for, to my great astonishment, I am as incapable of supernatural recollection as if I had never known what it was — and I could not possibly have resisted it if it had come. Don't worry: my head will get better by degrees. I take as much care of myself as I find I need to, and that is not a little — rather more, indeed, than is customary here. I shall not be able to practice prayer.

I want very much to get well again. As it is on your account, I think it is right I should, and I am of that sort of temperament that I must feel a thing to be right, or I shall worry about it. I find eating mutton so bad for me that I can take nothing but poultry. My whole trouble is weakness; I have been fasting since the Feast of the Cross in September, and at my age I find that trying. I am really irritated to discover I am so useless: this body of mine does me harm and keeps me from doing good.

(*Le* 171 to Lorenzo)

✦

This humor can subdue reason.... [I]f reason is wanting, madness results.... [T]o have to consider someone a rational person and deal with her as such even though she isn't is an unbearable burden.

(*F* 7.2)

That which interests these melancholic persons most is getting their own way, saying everything that comes to their lips, looking at the faults of others with which they hide their own, and finding rest in what gives them pleasure; in sum, they are like a person who cannot bear anyone who resists him. Well, if the passions go unmortified, and each passion seeks to get what it wants, what would happen if no one resisted them?

(*F* 7.3)

I repeat, as one who has seen and dealt with many persons having this affliction, that there is no other remedy for it than to make these persons submit in all the ways and means possible. If words do not suffice, use punishment; if light punishment is not enough, try heavy; if one month in the prison cell is not enough, try four months; no greater good can be done for their souls.

(*F* 7.4)

With this illness, very seldom are the afflicted cured, nor do they die from it but they come to lose their minds completely. ...They suffer more than death in themselves through afflictions, fantasies, and scruples, all of which they call temptations, and so they will have a great deal of merit. If they could come to understand that the illness is the cause of these, they would find much relief provided they paid no attention to them.

Indeed, I have great compassion for them, and it is also right that all those living with them have it.

(F 7.10)

As to what you call interior trials, the more you have of them the less notice you should take of them, for it is clear they are the result of an unstable imagination and weak condition, and, when the devil sees [anyone like] this, he has to add his mite as well. But do not be afraid, for St. Paul says that God will not permit us to be tempted above that which we are able (to bear); and, though you may think you are giving your consent, you are not, but will win merit from all this. Do get quite well again, for the love of God, and try to eat properly, and not to be alone, or to think of anything. Occupy yourself as well as you can and as you can. I wish I were with you, for it would do you good to hear a little entertaining chatter.

(Le 126 to María Bautista)

May the grace of the Holy Spirit be with you. I declare God seems to be allowing this poor man to try us so as to discover the extent of our charity. And really, brother, I have so little as far as he is concerned that it quite distresses me. For, even if he were not my brother at all, but only my neighbor, I ought to be moved by his necessity, and yet I feel most uncharitable towards him. I try to get over this feeling by reminding myself of what I ought to do to please God, and, once His Majesty enters into it, I find I would go to any lengths to help him. Were it not for that, I assure you I would not do a thing to hinder his going away, for I was so anxious to see him out of your house that the pleasure his departure gave me greatly exceeded my regrets at his trouble. So I beseech you, for love of Our Lord, do me the kindness not to take him back again into your house, however much he begs you to, and however great his need, and then I shall have some peace of mind again. For really, though he is sane enough in other respects, his desire to be with you is quite an insane one, which I understand from learned men is perfectly possible. And it is not the fault of his being at La Serna, for he was in the same condition before there was any question of his going there. What he has is a serious disease, and I have been dreadfully apprehensive of some disaster.

He says you are right to be cross with him but declares he cannot help himself. He knows quite well that he is doing himself harm, and must be very worried about it, but he says he has been feeling so bad about being here that he would rather die....

I think this unseasonable gloom you tell me you are feeling must be caused by Don Pedro's coming here; for God is very faithful. If he is insane, as I think he is in this respect, you are clearly the more strictly bound, by the law of perfection, to help him in so far as you can rather than allow him to go where he may die. You must give fewer alms to others, and bestow them on him, as your relationship to him obliges you to do....

You gave him two hundred reales for clothes, and a further sum for food, and there were other respects in which you helped him at home. They may have seemed inconsiderable, but such things cost more than perhaps you realize. What you have given him provides him with enough to pay for his board for the rest of the year, living wherever he likes. If you gave him two hundred reales a year, for his board, over and above the clothing allowance, he could stay with my sister, who, he says, has invited him to do so, or with Diego de Guzmán, who gave him a hundred reales, which he will spend on these journeys of his. If you give him anything next year, it is important you should not give it him all at once, but pay it by installments to whoever is boarding him, for my belief is he will not stay in any one place for long. It is a great pity. But, as long as he is not in your house, I think it is all to the good. Reckon part of what you give him as a present to me, which you would make me if you saw I was in need of it. I will accept it as if you gave it to me, and I only wish I could manage not to worry you about it. I assure you I have been wishing for a long time that Don Pedro were not in your house. I have been so sorry every now and then to see you tortured in this way....

Don Pedro had already spoken to me about the possibility you refer to of his living in one of our priories, but that is quite impracticable, for they do not receive laymen, and he would never stand the diet either. Even now he sends away the meat at the inn unless it is well cooked and highly seasoned, and makes do with a bit of pie. Whenever I can, I send him some little thing myself, but that is not very often. I don't know anyone who would put up with him and give him things just as he likes them.

A disposition like that is a dreadful thing — bad for him and for everyone. God give you the blessings I beseech Him for and preserve you from having to take him back home with you. But I am anxious that every other means of helping him shall be tried, and then, if he dies, neither you nor I will have any uneasy conscience.

(*Le* 316–17 to Lorenzo)

✣

Are You so in need, my Lord and my Love, that You would want to receive such poor company as mine, for I see by Your expression that You have been consoled by me? Well then, how is it Lord that the angels leave You and that even Your Father doesn't console You? If it's true, Lord, that You want to endure everything for me, what is this that I suffer for You? Of what am I complaining? I am already ashamed, since I have seen You in such a condition. I desire to suffer, Lord, all the trials that come to me and esteem them as a great good enabling me to imitate You in something. Let us walk together, Lord. Wherever You go, I will go; whatever you suffer, I will suffer.

(*W* 26.6)

Take up that cross.... In stumbling, in falling with your Spouse, do not withdraw from the cross or abandon it. Consider carefully the fatigue with which He walks and how much greater His trials are than those trials you suffer, however great you may want to paint them and no matter how much you grieve over them. You will come out consoled because you will see that they are something to be laughed at when compared to those of the Lord.

(*W* 26.7)

O Son of the Eternal Father, Jesus Christ, our Lord, true King of all! What did You leave in the world? What could we, your descendants, inherit from You? What did You possess, my Lord, but trials, sufferings, and dishonors? You had nothing but a wooden beam on which to swallow the painfully difficult drink of death. In sum, my God, it does not fit those of us who want to be your true children, and hold on to their inheritance, to flee suffering. Your heraldry consists of five wounds. Courage, then, my daughters; this must be our badge if we are to inherit His kingdom. Not with rest, not with favors, not with honors, not with riches will that which He bought with so much blood be gained. O illustrious people! Open your eyes for the love of God; behold that the true knights of Jesus Christ and the princes of His Church, a St. Peter and a St. Paul, did not follow the road you follow. Do you think perhaps there will be a new road for you? Do not believe it.

(*F* 10.11)

O true Lord and my Glory! How delicate and extremely heavy a cross You have prepared for those who reach this state! "Delicate" because it is pleasing; "heavy" because there come times when there is no capacity to bear it.... When it recalls that it hasn't served You in anything and that by living it can serve You, it would want to carry a much heavier cross and never die until the end of the world. It finds no rest in anything except in doing You some small service.

(*L* 16.5)

God gives contemplatives much greater trials. Thus, since He leads them along a rough and uneven path and at times they think they are lost and must return to begin again, His Majesty needs to give them sustenance, and not water but wine so that in their inebriation they will not understand what they are suffering and will be able to endure it.... [W]hen those of the active life see the contemplative favored a little, they think there is nothing else to the contemplative's life than receiving favors. Well, I say that perhaps these active persons couldn't endure one day of the kind the contemplative endures.

(*W* 18.2–3)

Even though the standard-bearer doesn't fight in the battle, he doesn't for that reason fail to walk in great danger; and interiorly he must do more work than anyone. Since he carries the flag, he cannot defend himself; and even though they cut him to pieces he must not let it out of his hands. So it is with contemplatives: they must keep the flag of humility raised and suffer all the blows they receive without returning any. Their duty is to suffer as Christ did, to hold high the cross, not to let it out of their hand whatever the dangers they see themselves in, nor let any weakness in suffering be seen in them; for this reason they are given so honorable an office. The contemplative must be careful about what he is doing, for if he lets go of the flag the battle will be lost.

(*W* 18.5)

One day the Lord told me: "You always desire trials, and on the other hand you refuse them. I dispose things in conformity with what I know is your will and not in conformity with your sensual nature and weakness. Take courage, since you see how I help you. I have desired that you win this crown."

(*T* 11)

Don't desire joy but suffering. O true Lord and my King! I'm still not ready for suffering if Your sovereign hand and greatness do not favor me, but with these I shall be able to do all things.

(*S* 6.3)

There is no other reason for living than to suffer trials, and this is what I most willingly beg of God. Sometimes I say earnestly to Him: "Lord, either to die or to suffer; I don't ask anything else for myself." I am consoled to hear the clock strike, for at the passing away of that hour of life it seems to me that I am drawing a little closer to the vision of God.

(L 40.20)

Your will, Lord, be done in me in every way and manner that You, my Lord, want. If You want it to be done with trials, strengthen me and let them come; if with persecutions, ill-nesses, dishonors, and a lack of life's necessities, here I am; I will not turn away, my Father, nor is it right that I turn my back on You.

(W 32.10)

❖

Since His Majesty can make one's strength increase in payment for the little that one determines to do for Him, He will give so many trials and persecutions and illnesses that a poor man won't know himself.

This happened to me when I was quite young. Sometimes I would say, "Oh, Lord, I didn't want so much." But His Majesty gave strength and patience in such a way that even now I am amazed at how I was able to suffer, and I would not exchange those trials for all the world's treasures.

(SS 6.1–2)

There is no remedy in this tempest but to wait for the mercy of God. For at an unexpected time, with one word alone or a chance happening, He so quickly calms the storm that it seems there had not been even as much as a cloud in that soul, and it remains filled with sunlight and much more consolation. And like one who has escaped from a dangerous battle and been victorious, it comes out praising our Lord; for it was He who fought for the victory. It knows very clearly that it did not fight, for all the weapons with which it could have defended itself are seen to be, it seems, in the hands of its enemies. Thus, it knows clearly its wretchedness and the very little we of ourselves can do if the Lord abandons us.

(*IC* 6.1.10)

This water from heaven often comes when the gardener is least expecting it. True, in the beginning it almost always occurs after a long period of mental prayer. The Lord comes to take this tiny bird from one degree to another and to place it in the nest so that it may have repose. Since He has seen it fly about for a long time, striving with the intellect and the will and all its strength to see God and please Him, He desires to reward it even in this life. And what a tremendous reward; one moment is enough to repay all the trials that can be suffered in life!

(*L* 18.9)

It is a great thing to have experienced the friendship and favor He shows toward those who journey on this road and how He takes care of almost all the expenses.

I'm not surprised that those who have not experienced this want the assurance of some gain for themselves. Well, you already know there is the hundredfold even in this life and that the Lord says, "ask, and you will receive." If you don't believe His Majesty in the sections of His gospel that insure this gain, it will be of little benefit, Sisters, for me to break my head in trying to tell you about it.

(*W* 23.5–6)

❖

May the grace of the Holy Spirit be with your Charities, my sisters and daughters. I assure you I have never loved you as much as I do now and you have never been bound to serve Our Lord as much as you are now, when He is granting you the great blessing of being able to taste something of the meaning of His Cross and to realize something of the keen sense of desolation which His Majesty felt as He hung upon it. It was a happy day for you when you entered your house, since He was preparing you a period of such good fortune. I envy you tremendously:

truth to tell, when I learned of all the ups and downs you had suffered — and they took the greatest trouble to explain it all to me — and of how attempts were made to turn you out of your house, and various other details, there came to me the deepest inward joy, for I saw that, without your having crossed the sea, Our Lord has been pleased to open up for you mines of eternal treasures. I trust in His Majesty you will grow very rich, and share your wealth with those of us who are here. For I have great confidence in His mercy that He will grant you the grace to bear everything and to offend Him in nothing. So, if you feel it all deeply, do not be distressed: it is the Lord Who is being pleased to make you realize that you are not capable of as much as you thought you were when you longed so much to suffer.

Courage, courage, my daughters. Remember, God gives no one more troubles than he is able to bear, and He is with those who are in tribulation. . . .

Oh, what a good time this is for you to harvest the fruits of the resolutions you have made to serve Our Lord! Remember, it is often His pleasure to test our actions and see if they match our resolutions and our words. Let the Virgin's daughters, your own sisters, see you coming honorably out of this great persecution. If you help yourselves, the good Jesus will help you; for, though He is asleep on the sea, when the storm rises He will still the winds. His pleasure is that we should ask Him for what we need, and so much does He love us that He is always seeking ways to help us. Blessed be His name for ever. Amen, Amen, Amen.

In all our houses, the nuns are continually commending you to God, so I trust that, in His goodness, He will soon put things right. Try to be cheerful, and reflect that, when all is said, it is very little that you are suffering for so good a God, Who endured so much for us: you have not even shed any of your blood for Him yet. You are among your sisters, not in Algiers.

(Le 264 to Seville Convent)

Chapter 6

Personal Passionate Presence

Prayer in my opinion is nothing else than an intimate sharing between friends; it means taking time frequently to be alone with Him who we know loves us.

(L 8.5)

Teresa is imaginative in her descriptions of prayer. With characteristic drama, she calls it a matter of life and death. She suffered serious regression when she abandoned prayer for over a year in midlife. So she cautions us against the same stupid mistake, which she says puts us "right in hell." When we practice prayer, we are like those who watch the bullfight safely from the stands, instead of right in front of the bull's horns.

Prayer is like growing a garden, Teresa explains, in one of her classic images. We grow in prayer through four degrees, similar to watering the garden — from the laborious effort of drawing water from a well through the great blessing of watching rain soak the ground without any work on our part. In a dry season, we must make the effort to use the well, the waterwheel, or irrigation.

Watering with buckets from the well is the beginning stage: vocal and meditative prayer requiring considerable effort. The waterwheel stage is the beginning of "infused" graces we cannot acquire on our own, bringing quiet and recollection. When the water begins to irrigate the garden from a river or stream, we are happily disquieted: even intoxicated by a kind of holy madness. We are eager and ready to share our joy in work and service.

131

When the rain falls, we are ecstatic over our union with God, our Spouse, in the heights of contemplation, which makes us capable of the most heroic deeds. In this high degree, prayer is not work but glory.

Meditation and Contemplation

It can be difficult to understand Teresian prayer unless we know what Teresa means by the three faculties of the human person — will, memory, and intellect. In *The Interior Castle*, as Teresa moves through the seven dwelling places and the four ways of watering the garden, she describes what happens to these three faculties in terms of how "captivated" they are by God. In the lower stages of prayer, only the will is occupied, the "captive of its lover." The intellect and memory still have a life of their own and "wander" distractedly. As we grow in prayer, these two faculties begin to "sleep." That means they are occasionally absorbed in God, but not yet united. They still "flit from one thing to the other like little moths at night." In the highest degree of prayer, all three of these faculties are captivated, united, or "suspended," to use the classic term. Another classic description is "ligature." Put in more contemporary terminology, this simply means that as we grow in prayer, we move from distraction to concentration and heightened awareness of God. At first we become stilled because we like it. Then we become stilled by awe and wonder before the glory of God.

We must remember that Teresa sometimes uses the terms "imagination," "memory," "mind," and "intellect" interchangeably, so we mustn't bog down in her terminology. Her inconsistency has been the despair of scholars for centuries. Teresa gets more precise as she develops through the years. But it's far easier to make clear distinctions on paper than in real life. Prayer by nature, as an integral part of the dynamic flow of life, can't be bound by mental concepts. There is never any clear demarcation between the various stages of growth. We should use categories if they help and ignore them if they hinder us.

What do we do when the well runs dry, when we go to fetch water and there is none — no interior tenderness, no feelings of devotion, no consolation, only dryness, distaste, aridity, and relentless, vapid, unrewarding effort? We go to prayer, let the pail down into the well, and come up with nothing. This is a common experience at the beginning of the journey of prayer, and we must not give up.

Teresa counsels us with her incomparable compassion and common sense. This dryness in prayer may have some natural cause: a change in the weather, fatigue, illness, or some other bodily disorder. We mustn't be too hard on ourselves but choose some simple alternative: change the hour of prayer, do some spiritual reading or some work of charity, engage in holy conversation, go to the country. Dryness is inevitable.

In *The Way of Perfection*, Teresa no longer uses poetic imagery to discuss degrees of prayer but resorts to more "technical" language. She shows how vocal prayer must really be mental prayer that in turn can lead to contemplative prayer.

Teresa despised "womanish" and superstitious prayers: "May God deliver us from foolish devotions," she cried. But she prized the recitation of robust vocal prayers, particularly those that come from the mouth of the Lord himself. She unpacks the meaning of the Our Father for us in mystical terms and marvels that in the few words of this prayer we get an in-depth treatise on prayer and high contemplation, from the beginning stages to mental prayer, through the prayer of quiet to the prayer of union.

Teresa insists that we refuse to be satisfied with merely pronouncing the words to traditional prayers. If vocal prayer is not accompanied by mental prayer, that is, if we recite the words to vocal prayers mechanically and routinely, letting our minds think of other things instead of understanding whom we are speaking to, then vocal prayer is no prayer at all. For we are obliged to pray with attention.

It may help us to use the term "meditative prayer" rather than "mental prayer." For Teresa, this prayer is a meditation or a "consideration": Who am I? To whom am I speaking? What is an appropriate mode of address? In meditative prayer, we center our minds on the presence of the one to whom we are relating.

Teresa shows us how we can be raised to high contemplation in the midst of vocal prayer prayed meditatively. She gives us an exquisite description of perfect contemplation: a gratuitous enkindling in love, an understanding without understanding, without the noise of words, and without any effort on our part.

The Wandering Mind

Teresa grapples frequently in her writings with the instability, turmoil, and rebellion of the imagination. (Remember: she uses the terms "imagination," "mind," "intellect," and sometimes "memory" interchangeably.) She calls the scattered mind a wild horse, running here, running there, always restless. She compares her own distracted mind to a bird frantically flying about, not knowing where to light. At one point she becomes so disgusted with herself, she says: "Sometimes I want to die in that I cannot cure this wandering of the intellect!" God consoled her by telling her she could never avoid it completely in this life, and Teresa did learn how to cope creatively with the problem.

We cannot allow the mind to wander without making *some* effort to control it. But this effort must be gentle, not forceful, for the more arduous the effort, the more the mind rebels. Here, as in all her advice, Teresa recommends a light touch — and a touch of humor. Let the "millclapper" of the mind "go clacking on." Pay no more attention to the intellect than you would to a madman. Laugh at it the way you laugh at a fool. We must not grow anxious but allow the will to remain calm at the center.

Teresa's method of calming and recollecting the wandering mind may be summed up in the traditional term "the practice of the presence of God" or in the more contemporary expression "personal passionate presence."

In Teresa's day, as well as our own, a common form of meditation, to prepare for prayer, was discursive reflection: using the intellect itself to reason from one idea to the next, from one thought to another, proceeding logically and methodically point by point. Teresa criticizes herself for being incapable of doing this and blames her dull mind, bad memory, and poor imagination. But God was actually leading her by another more intuitive path.

Teresa's path is laborious and painful. If we cannot work discursively with the intellect, the battle with distracting thoughts is ferocious. This is why we may need to use images, a book, or "the book of nature." On the plus side, however, this path helps us advance more quickly because we advance in love.

In her *Life*, Teresa describes her own struggle to learn how to focus and pray. In *The Way of Perfection*, chapters 26, 28, and 29, we benefit from that struggle as Teresa outlines her method of recollecting the mind. She tells us not to use our intellects to think discursively about Jesus, but simply to make ourselves aware of his presence as our friend and constant companion. "Simply look at Him," she says over and over again. If you're joyful, look at him risen from the tomb. If you're sad, behold him in his passion: in the garden, bound to the column, burdened with the cross. We must get used to this practice, no matter how long it takes. What's our hurry? This method of keeping Christ present is beneficial in all stages of growth, and we should begin, continue, and end with it.

We call this personal passionate presence a spiritual *practice* because it is something we can work at and acquire ourselves. But there is another kind of quiet presence that is given gratuitously, infused, or "supernatural." We cannot achieve it by our own effort, no matter how hard we try, but our own efforts to be recollected in the presence of God help *dispose* us for it. This deeper, more infused recollection is described in chapter 3 of the Fourth Dwelling Place in the *Castle*. We move from it into what is called the prayer of quiet, which Teresa discusses in chapter 31 of the *Way* and chapter 2 of the Fourth Dwelling Place. There are degrees of quiet and peace as we grow in the prayer of presence, or as Teresa puts it, "a more and a less." All we have to remember as we proceed through these degrees is that we are moving into deeper and deeper realms of recollection, stillness, and effortlessness — whether we are talking in terms of water, the way, fire, the castle, quiet, or presence.

In the infused prayer of recollection, we experience a gentle drawing inward, like a hedgehog curling up or a turtle drawing into its shell. We cannot bring this about ourselves but must wait for God to grant it. What should be our response to this favor? Since we cannot induce it, we must "beg like the needy poor before a rich and great emperor, and then lower our eyes and wait with humility." We will be tempted to try and prolong this quiet by not even daring to take a breath. This is foolish, Teresa chides us, because we cannot control it any more than we can make the sun rise and set. But we can help nurture it. How? By a *gentle* working with the intellect to help control its aimless wandering.

For even in this stage of quiet, which Teresa also calls "spiritual delight," the intellect wanders. This is a transitional stage in the Fourth Dwelling Place, where natural and supernatural, acquired and infused, meditative and mystical intermingle. As we have already seen, sheer effort alone cannot stop the mind from wandering. It continues to move from one extreme to another, like a fool unable to rest in anything. Teresa says that when we try to stop it ourselves and try to induce this prayer of quiet, we attempt the impossible: the imagination becomes more restless through the effort we make not to think of anything at all.

This is such a crucial point that Teresa deals with it in all three of her major spiritual writings. In the *Life*, she says that if we take it upon ourselves to suspend all thought and move into this more infused quiet, we will be left like "cold simpletons" in a dry desert. In the *Way*, she insists that we make the intellect "work a little, although so gently that it almost doesn't feel its effort." Her emphasis is on *gentle*, the way we blow on a candle to enkindle it again when the flame begins to die out. If we blow too hard, we put the candle out. In *The Interior Castle*, she tells us she's finally explaining this with the greatest clarity, and so she becomes most emphatic: "If His Majesty has not begun to absorb us, I cannot understand how the mind can be stopped. There's no way of doing so without bringing about more harm than good. . . . [T]hose in favor of stopping the mind have never given me a reason for submitting to what they say."

Teresa then goes on to justify her strong position. The intellect will not truly rest until God has so "awakened" love in the soul that even the intellect cannot resist and falls captive. We should simply let the intellect go its way and surrender ourselves into the arms of love.

It is imperative to understand and apply this teaching in our own day because we seem to have fallen into the very trap Teresa warns us against so vehemently: quietism instead of quiet. Many contemporary spiritual practices for calming the overactive intellect focus on emptying or voiding the mind by breath control, counting, or the use of mantras. Teresa provides a helpful critique of these practices and explains why so many Christians get stuck in them: instead of reaching true quiet, they simply end up in a vacuum, like "dunces," incapable of growing into higher degrees of contemplative prayer. They need to continue working gently with the intellect if they are to be enkindled more in love and are to rediscover the presence and humanity of Christ.

The essence of Teresian prayer is summed up in one of her favorite maxims: "The important thing is not to think much but to love much." Why? Because the soul is not the mind. Not everyone is capable of thinking discursively; but everyone is capable of loving. When we pray, we should do whatever best stirs us to love. If we can't muster up a good thought, we shouldn't kill ourselves trying, because it doesn't matter.

As we grow in prayer, we grow in love. God gives us a little spark of love as a sign that we are chosen for great things, if we will dispose ourselves to receive them. If we do not extinguish this tiny spark, God will enkindle it into a conflagration.

Teresa gives special advice to more intellectual personalities who may be tempted to spend too much time in discursive reflection because it is their nature to work with concepts. They should change their diet, should not wear themselves out composing syllogisms, and should simply put themselves in the personal passionate presence of Christ.

The Real Presence

"We are not angels but we have a body," Teresa points out with her characteristic practicality. Therefore, she insists, it is very destructive for us to think that we can grow in the spiritual life if we forgo the humanity of Christ.

In Teresa's time, as in our own, certain schools of meditation and prayer taught the necessity of ridding ourselves of all corporeal images. Teresa attempts politely to be open to this position and says she won't contradict it; then she turns around and does.

Chapter 22 of the *Life* is a pivotal Teresian essay on the humanity of Christ as the means to the most sublime contemplation. All our trouble comes from not keeping our eyes on him. In more advanced stages of mystical prayer, God does lead us beyond corporeal images of Christ. But few actually advance to this stage. And to let go of these images ourselves — intentionally, methodically, and prematurely — is a serious mistake that retards our growth.

Teresa calls Jesus our true friend and best example, an excellent leader who went before us and shows us the way in all things. We should always desire to live in his presence even if we are at the summit of contemplation. The most sacred humanity of Christ is not to be counted in a balance with other corporeal things from which we must be detached. If we let go of this sacred humanity before the proper time, when God takes it away, we will be left floating in the air and as dry as sticks; instead of advancing we will slip backward and regress.

Devoted as she was to the humanity of Jesus, Teresa was also passionately devoted to the Real Presence of Christ in the Blessed Sacrament, disguised under the appearance of simple bread and wine so that we might bear his glory. Teresa laughed at those who said they wished they had lived at the time Christ walked in the world. She wondered what more they wanted, since in the Blessed Sacrament we have him "just as truly present as He was then."

Teresa was so overwhelmed by the majesty of God concealed

in something as small as the Host, it made her hair stand on end. It was a great consolation to her to found so many convents with chapels so that Jesus Christ, true God and true man, could be present in the Blessed Sacrament in many more places. It tormented her that during the Protestant Reformation so many churches were destroyed and the Blessed Sacrament desecrated. For her this meant crucifying Jesus all over again, and her heart could not bear it. "Make the sea calm!" she prayed ardently: "May this ship, which is the Church, not always have to journey in a tempest like this."

When she made her foundation in Medina del Campo, the walls of the new chapel were falling down and the Blessed Sacrament was exposed to the street. Teresa was distraught and put some men in charge of keeping watch. But she was so worried that they might fall asleep, she herself arose during the night to keep watch through a window.

Many of Teresa's most powerful experiences of God occurred just after receiving Communion. This is a very sacred time, and she scolds us for not being attentive enough and for receiving casually, mindlessly, and routinely. When Teresa received Communion, she believed that Jesus entered her poor home, and she threw herself at his feet like the Magdalene. She urges us to be equally as attentive. Approaching the Eucharist is like approaching a fire: even though the fire may be a large one, it cannot warm us well if we turn away from it.

Meditation

In the following texts, Teresa describes the danger of abandoning prayer; the activity of the will, intellect, and memory during prayer; and the importance of remaining humble and faithful during periods of aridity. Then she describes the relationship between vocal, meditative, and contemplative prayer without the "noise of words." She comforts us by sharing her own struggles with distractions at prayer and urges us to use reading as an aid to calming and recollecting a wild imagination or intellect. She advises us not to grow anxious and to keep our sense of humor.

In the next series of texts, we see concrete evidence of Teresa's method of meditation — personal passionate presence — especially in the example of Jesus in the Garden of Gethsemane. This leads to the importance of the humanity of Jesus and her insistence on loving instead of thinking — provided we understand what love is. We then move to Teresa's sublime meditations on the Blessed Sacrament and the necessity of receiving Holy Communion mindfully and not routinely.

In conclusion, Teresa writes to Gracián and explains how the most potent prayer is characterized by virtue and effective action, not consolation. In another comforting passage, she explains how our very suffering is already prayer.

Teresian Texts: Personal Passionate Presence

During the time in which I was without prayer my life was much worse. Look at the good remedy the devil gave me and the charming humility — the great disquiet within me. But how could I quiet my soul? It was losing its calm.... Through the practice of prayer and spiritual reading I knew the truths and the bad road I was following and often entreated the Lord with many tears.

(*L* 19.11–12)

In this prayer [second water] the faculties are gathered within so as to enjoy that satisfaction with greater delight. But they are not lost, nor do they sleep. Only the will is occupied in such a way that, without knowing how, it becomes captive; it merely consents to God allowing Him to imprison it as one who well knows how to be the captive of its lover. O Jesus and my Lord! How valuable is Your love to us here! It holds our love so bound that it doesn't allow it the freedom during that time to love anything else but You.

(*L* 14.2)

What I call noise is running about with the intellect looking for many words and reflections so as to give thanks for this gift and piling up one's sins and faults in order to see that the gift is unmerited. Everything is motion here; the intellect is representing, and the memory hurrying about. For certainly these faculties tire me out from time to time; and although I have a poor memory, I cannot subdue it. The will calmly and wisely must understand that one does not deal well with God by force and that our efforts are like the careless use of large pieces of wood which smother this little spark.

(L 15.6)

This gardener helps Christ carry the cross and reflects that the Lord lived with it all during His life. He doesn't desire the Lord's kingdom here below or ever abandon prayer. And so he is determined, even though this dryness may last for his whole life, not to let Christ fall with the cross. The time will come when the Lord will repay him all at once. He doesn't fear that the labor is being wasted. He is serving a good Master whose eyes are upon him. He doesn't pay any attention to bad thoughts.

(L 11.10)

Oh, humility, humility!...Anyone who makes such an issue of this dryness is a little lacking in humility....Let us prove ourselves, or let the Lord prove us, for He knows well how to do this even though we often don't want to understand it....Out of dryness...draw humility — and not disquiet....We are fonder of consolations than we are of the cross. Test us, Lord—for you know the truth—so that we may know ourselves.

(IC 3.1.7–8)

❖

The door of entry to this castle is prayer and reflection. I don't mean to refer to mental more than vocal prayer, for since vocal prayer is prayer it must be accompanied by reflection. A prayer in which a person is not aware of whom he is speaking to, what he is asking, who it is who is asking and of whom,

I do not call prayer however much the lips move. Sometimes it will be so without this reflection, provided that the soul has these reflections at other times. Nonetheless, anyone who has the habit of speaking before God's majesty as though he were speaking to a slave, without being careful to see how he is speaking, but saying whatever comes into his head and whatever he has learned from saying at other times, in my opinion is not praying.

(*IC* 1.1.7)

The soul understands that without the noise of words this divine Master is teaching it by suspending its faculties, for if they were to be at work they would do harm rather than bring benefit. They are enjoying without understanding how they are enjoying. The soul is being enkindled in love, and it doesn't understand how it loves. It knows that it enjoys what it loves, but it doesn't know how. It clearly understands that this joy is not a joy the intellect obtains merely through desire. The will is enkindled without understanding how. But as soon as it can understand something, it sees that this good cannot be merited or gained through all the trials one can suffer on earth. This good is a gift from the Lord of earth and heaven, who, in sum, gives according to who He is. What I have described, daughters, is perfect contemplation.

(*W* 25.2)

❖

On the vigil of St. Lawrence, just after receiving Communion, my mental faculties were so scattered and distracted I couldn't help myself, and I began to envy those who live in deserts and to think that since they don't hear or see anything they are free of this wandering of the mind. I heard: "You are greatly mistaken, daughter; rather, the temptations of the devil there are stronger; be patient, for as long as you live, a wandering mind cannot be avoided."

(*T* 39.1)

In all those years, except for the time after Communion, I never dared to begin prayer without a book. For my soul was as fearful of being without it during prayer as it would have been should it have had to do battle with a lot of people. With this recourse, which was like a partner or a shield by which to sustain the blows of my many thoughts, I went about consoled. For dryness was not usually felt, but it was always felt when I was without a book. Then my soul was thrown into confusion and my thoughts ran wild. With a book I began to collect them, and my soul was drawn to recollection. And many times just opening the book was enough; at other times I read a little and at others a great deal.

(*L* 4.9)

While writing this, I'm thinking about what's going on in my head with the great noise there that I mentioned in the beginning. It makes it almost impossible for me to write what I was ordered to. It seems as if there are in my head many rushing rivers and that these waters are hurtling downward, and many little birds and whistling sounds, not in the ears but in the upper part of the head.... For all this turmoil in my head doesn't hinder prayer or what I am saying, but the soul is completely taken up in its quiet, love, desires, and clear knowledge.

(*IC* 4.1.10)

This intellect is so wild that it doesn't seem to be anything else than a frantic madman no one can tie down; nor am I master of it long enough to keep it calm for the space of a Creed. Sometimes I laugh at myself and know my misery, and I look at this madman and leave it alone to see what it does; and — glory to God — it surprisingly enough never turns to evil but to indifferent things; to whether there is anything to do here or there or over yonder.... [S]o I say to the Lord: "When, my God, will I finally see my soul joined together in Your praise, so that all its faculties may enjoy You? Do not permit, Lord, that it be broken any longer in pieces, for it only seems that each piece goes its own way."

(L 30.16)

[The will] laughs at the intellect as at a fool when this intellect — or mind, to explain myself better — goes off to the more foolish things of the world. The will remains in its quietude, for the intellect will come and go. In this prayer the will is the ruler and the powerful one. It will draw the intellect after itself without your being disturbed. And if the will should desire to draw the intellect by force of arms, the strength it has against the intellect will be lost.... As the saying goes, whoever tries to grasp too much loses everything.

(W 31.10)

Whoever experiences the affliction these distractions cause will see that they are not his fault; he should not grow anxious, which makes things worse, or tire himself trying to put order into something that at the time doesn't have any, that is, his mind. He should just pray as best he can; or even not pray, but like a sick person strive to bring some relief to his soul; let him occupy himself in other works of virtue. This advice now is for persons who are careful.

(W 24.5)

❖

This is the method of prayer I then used: since I could not reflect discursively with the intellect, I strove to picture Christ within me, and it did me greater good — in my opinion — to picture Him in those scenes where I saw Him more alone. It seemed to me that being alone and afflicted, as a person in need, He had to accept me. I had many simple thoughts like these.

The scene of His prayer in the garden, especially, was a comfort to me; I strove to be His companion there. If I could, I thought of the sweat and agony He had undergone in that place. I desired to wipe away the sweat He so painfully experienced, but I recall that I never dared to actually do it, since my sins appeared to me so serious. I remained with Him as long as my thoughts allowed me to, for there were many distractions that tormented me. Most nights, for many years before going to bed when I commended myself to God in preparation for sleep, I always pondered for a little while this episode of the prayer in the garden. I did this even before I was a nun.

(*L* 9.4)

I had such little ability to represent things with my intellect that if I hadn't seen the things my imagination was not of use to me, as it is to other persons who can imagine things and thus recollect themselves. I could only think about Christ as He was as man, but never in such a way that I could picture Him within myself no matter how much I read about His beauty or how many images I saw of Him. I was like one who is blind or in darkness; he speaks with a person and sees that person is with him because he knows with certainty that he is there (I mean he understands and believes he is there, but does not see him); such was the case with me when I thought of our Lord. This was the reason I liked images so much. Unfortunate are those who through their own fault lose this great good. It indeed appears that they do not love the Lord, for if they loved Him they would rejoice to see a portrait of Him, just as here on earth it really gives joy to see one whom you deeply love.

(*L* 9.6)

I'm not asking you now that you think about Him or that you draw out a lot of concepts or make long and subtle reflections with your intellect. I'm not asking you to do anything more than look at Him.... If you are joyful, look at Him as risen. Just imagining how He rose from the tomb will bring you joy. The brilliance! The beauty! The majesty! How victorious! How joyful! Indeed, like one coming forth from a battle where he has gained a great kingdom!... If you are experiencing trials or are sad, behold Him on the way to the garden: what great affliction He bore in His soul; for having become suffering itself, He tells us about it and complains of it. Or behold Him bound to the column, filled with pain, with all His flesh torn into pieces for the great love He bears you; so much suffering, persecuted by some, spit on by others, denied by His friends, abandoned by them, with no one to defend Him, frozen from the cold, left so alone that you can console each other. Or behold Him burdened with the cross, for they didn't even let Him take a breath. He will look at you with those eyes so beautiful and compassionate, filled with tears; He will forget His sorrows so as to console you in yours, merely because you yourselves go to Him to be consoled, and you turn your head to look at Him.

(*W* 26.3–5)

Those of you who cannot engage in much discursive reflection with the intellect or keep your mind from distraction, get used to this practice! Get used to it! See, I know that you can do this; for I suffered many years from the trial — and it is a very great one — of not being able to quiet the mind in anything. But I know that the Lord does not leave us so abandoned; for if we humbly ask Him for this friendship, He will not deny it to us. And if we cannot succeed in one year, we will succeed later. Let's not regret the time that is so well spent. Who's making us hurry?

(*W* 26.2)

✤

I have run into some for whom it seems the whole business lies in thinking. If they can keep their mind much occupied in God, even though great effort is exerted, they at once think they are spiritual. If, on the contrary, without being able to avoid it, they become distracted, even if for the sake of good things, they then become disconsolate and think they are lost. . . . I do not deny that it is a favor from the Lord if someone is able to be always meditating on His works, and it is good that one strive to do so. However, it must be understood that not all imaginations are by their nature capable of this meditating, but all souls are capable of loving. . . . The soul is not the mind, nor is the will directed by thinking, for this would be very unfortunate. Hence, the soul's progress does not lie in thinking much but in loving much.

(*F* 5.2)

This prayer, then, is a little spark of the Lord's true love which He begins to enkindle in the soul.... [T]his little spark cannot be acquired. Yet, this nature of ours is so eager for delights that it tries everything; but it is quickly left cold because however much it may desire to light the fire and obtain this delight, it doesn't seem to be doing anything else than throwing water on it and killing it.... If we don't extinguish it, through our own fault, it is what will begin to enkindle the large fire that (as I shall mention in its place) throws forth flames of the greatest love of God.

(*L* 15.4)

They should not pass the whole time thinking. For although discursive reflection is very meritorious, they don't seem to realize that since their prayer is delightful there should ever be a Sunday or a time in which one is not working; but they think such time is lost. I consider this loss a great gain. But, as I have said, they should put themselves in the presence of Christ and, without tiring the intellect, speak with and delight in Him and not wear themselves out in composing syllogisms.

(*L* 13.11)

The important thing is not to think much but to love much; and so do that which best stirs you to love. Perhaps we don't know what love is. I wouldn't be very surprised because it doesn't consist in great delight but in desiring with strong determination to please God in everything, in striving, insofar as possible, not to offend Him, and in asking Him for the advancement of the honor and glory of His Son.

(*IC* 4.1.7)

It is fitting for souls, however spiritual, to take care not to flee from corporeal things to the extent of thinking that even the most sacred humanity causes harm. Some quote what the Lord said to His disciples that it was fitting that He go. I can't bear this. I would wager that He didn't say it to His most Blessed Mother, because she was firm in the faith; she knew He was God and man, and even though she loved Him more than they did, she did so with such perfection that His presence was a help rather than a hindrance.

(*IC* 6.7.14)

✦

If we were to approach the most Blessed Sacrament with great faith and love, once would be enough to leave us rich. How much richer from approaching so many times as we do. The trouble is we do so out of routine, and it shows.

(*SS* 3.13)

Be with Him willingly; don't lose so good an occasion for conversing with Him as is the hour after having received Communion.... If you immediately turn your thoughts to other things, if you pay no attention and take no account of the fact that He is within you, how will He be able to reveal Himself to you? This, then, is a good time for our Master to teach us, and for us to listen to Him, kiss His feet because He wanted to teach us, and beg Him not to leave.

(*W* 34.10)

After having received the Lord, since you have the Person Himself present, strive to close the eyes of the body and open those of the soul and look into your own heart. For I tell you, and tell you again, and would like to tell you many times that you should acquire the habit of doing this every time you receive Communion.

(*W* 34.12)

Especially after receiving Communion — for we know that He is present, since our faith tells us this — He reveals Himself as so much the lord of this dwelling that it seems the soul is completely dissolved; and it sees itself consumed in Christ. O my

Jesus! Who could make known the majesty with which You reveal Yourself! And, Lord of all the world and of the heavens, of a thousand other worlds and of numberless worlds, and of the heavens that You might create.

(*L* 28.8)

❖

The most potent and acceptable prayer is the prayer that leaves the best effects. I do not mean it must immediately fill the soul with desires; for, although such desires are good, they are sometimes not as good as our love of self makes us think. I should describe the best effects as those that are followed up by actions — when the soul not only desires the honor of God, but really strives for it, and employs the memory and understanding in considering how it may please Him and show its love for Him more and more.

Oh, that is real prayer — which cannot be said of a handful of consolations that do nothing but console ourselves. When the soul experiences these, they leave it weak and fearful and sensitive to what others think of it. I should never want any prayer that would not make the virtues grow within me. If with my prayer there come severe temptations and aridities and tribulations, and these leave me humbler, then I should consider it good prayer, for by the best prayer I mean that which is most pleasing to God. One must not think that a person who is suffering is not praying. He is offering up his sufferings to God, and many a time he is praying much more truly than one who goes away by himself and meditates his head off, and, if he has squeezed out a few tears, thinks that is prayer.

(*Le* 122 to Gracián)

Chapter 7

Intimacy and Ecstasy

Oh Love! How I would want to say this word everywhere. . . . He gives us permission to think that He, this true Lover, my Spouse and my Good, needs us.

(*SS* 4.11)

For Teresa, all life is relatedness — between persons and ultimately between persons and God. Therefore, prayer is not merely a practice but a presence, not an exercise but an ecstasy, not something we do but Someone we meet.

Prayer is an intimate sharing between friends. "Oh, what a good friend You make, my Lord!" Teresa often exclaims, overwhelmed when she learns that God seeks our friendship and "needs" our companionship. "Oh, compassion so measureless!" And yet we ungratefully forget this privilege and the source of our dignity.

Teresa uses the image of human friendship to describe our intimacy with God, who is indescribably close to us, intimately near, personally and passionately present. This love startles us. Most of us don't have the courage to embrace it. Courage? Yes! For just as earthly intimacy requires courage — to be vulnerable, found out, and *known* by the other — intimacy with God also requires courage.

If prayer is an intimate sharing between friends, it means "taking time frequently to be alone with Him who we know loves us" — just as we take time with our human friends. Our love for God grows when we understand that we can converse with the One who is human while still being divine. We can speak with God as a friend, even though he is Lord.

"My God is not at all touchy," Teresa tells us in one of her charming insights. "He doesn't bother about trifling things." She's chagrined but can't stop herself from speaking boldly to God, who listens attentively and puts up with her. Her prayer often takes the form of complaint or lament, and she encourages us to pray this way as well, since it is far better to complain to God than to other people.

Teresa complains about her bad health, her relentless hard work, and her miserable human weaknesses. She complains that Jesus loves Mary Magdalene more than herself. She complains that God allows her brother Agustín to be in a place where his spiritual life is jeopardized: "Were I, Lord, to see Your brother in this danger, what wouldn't I do to help him!" Reaching a veritable apogee in the *Life*, she complains outrageously that it's bad enough for God to keep her in this "miserable life" where she has to "eat and sleep and carry on business and talk with everyone," but then when she finally scrounges some little bit of time to pray, God "hides" from her.

Praise-Names

Teresa encourages us to speak with God as with a friend, a father, a brother, a lord, or a spouse — sometimes in one way, at other times in another. In her writings we find her speaking to God in all these different modes. She calls him our Model and Master, Good Teacher, True Virtue, and Eternal Wisdom. She gives God names of comfort: my Mercy, Hope, and Happiness, Redeemer Sweet, Wealth of the Poor, Good of All Goods, and Rest from All Pains. When she experiences divine power, she refers to God as Conqueror, Victor, Giant, the Strong One, and True Fortitude. Mindful of his grandeur, she calls God "His Majesty" more frequently than any other name. She also addresses him as Prince, Emperor, Lord, and Sacred King of Glory.

Her more intimate names include Guest, Companion, Most Loving Lamb, True Friend, and the Very Lord of Love. She often gets so carried away that she strings together a whole catalogue of extravagant epithets: "Majestic Sovereign, Unending Wisdom, Kindness pleasing to my soul"; "Consoler of the disconsolate and Cure for anyone who wants to be cured by You"; "O my God and my infinite Wisdom, measureless and boundless and beyond all the human and the angelic intellects! O love that loves me more than I can love myself or understand!" We all need to be this creative in finding appropriate praise-names for God.

We experience a significant turning point in the intimacy of our prayer when *the* Lord becomes *my* Lord. Teresa speaks frequently of *my* Jesus, *my* heavenly Father, *my* King, *my* Spouse. The words "my" and "mine" do not signify possession but *relation*, although in God's infinite largesse, he seems to allow us to "possess" him in the intimate way lovers possess one another.

Spousal intimacy clearly dominates Teresa's life. She speaks of God as her Spouse, Bridegroom, and Lover. She throws herself into his arms, holds his hand, and kisses his mouth, calling his heavenly breasts "better and more delightful than wine." This is the ancient and revered tradition of the church known as "bridal mysticism." Teresa is one of its chief models and proponents.

Marriage today is a tragedy and a travesty, with too little evidence of fidelity. But we should not for this reason belittle Teresa's frequent use of the marriage image to describe our relationship to God. For Teresa, marriage is not a contract but an embrace. As we move through the interior castle, we grow in our intimate love-life with God. In the Fifth Dwelling Place we meet; in the Sixth we are betrothed; in the Seventh our marriage is consummated. Teresa describes the union of spiritual marriage in a magnificent cascade of water and light imagery: a downpour of rain into a swelling river, a little stream entering the mighty ocean, a bright light beaming into a room through separate windows and becoming one.

Teresa knows that this kind of talk is madness. When our faith is dead, we do not dare to speak this foolishness. But when our faith is alive and we are dying with love, we can't help ourselves. Teresa uses ecstatic language to describe a "holy madness," "glorious foolishness," "divine intoxication," and "heavenly inebriation" where we are brought into the wine cellar along with the Bride in *The Song of Songs*. The whole person experiences comfort — interiorly and exteriorly. It's as though a sweet ointment with a powerful fragrance were poured into the marrow of our bones. No earthly pleasure comes close to it. The joy is so great, it sometimes seems that the soul is at the very point of leaving the body. This is the literal meaning of ecstasy: *ek-statis*, standing outside of ourselves.

Teresa highly prized reason, learning, and the towering work of the intellect. But at this point, she expresses disgust over those who will not forgo reason and surrender their intellects to a "Higher Power." She criticizes those who cannot "let go and let God" but insist on being rational, precise, and in control. In a marvelous paragraph expressing the ineffability of this level of prayer — a level at which we cannot even remember a scriptural passage we might just have read — Teresa uses the word "understand" seven times and ends by saying she doesn't at all understand what she understands! This is another classic description of perfect contemplation as "understanding without understanding."

Teresa uses the terms "ecstasy," "rapture," "transport," and "elevation" or "flight of the spirit" almost synonymously. Whereas the experience of union with God is felt only interiorly, these other experiences produce their effects exteriorly as well. Flight of the spirit is substantially the same as rapture, only it occurs more swiftly.

In all her descriptions of ecstasy, Teresa refers in one way or another to being carried away. "The Lord gathers up the soul" or "raises it completely out of itself"; a "mighty eagle" carries it "aloft on its wings." Sometimes the rapture results in levitation: the body mirrors the experience of the soul and actually leaves the ground. Teresa found this humiliating and distressing. She fought against it with all her might and even asked her friends to sit on top of her as she stretched herself out on the floor. Levitation was extremely rare for her, occurring early in her mystical life and only a few times later when she was too weak to preclude it.

True and False Ecstasy

Teresa explains in detail what happens to the body in ecstasy. But what matters far more to her are the interior effects: humility in the face of God's majesty, self-forgetfulness, detachment, deep repentance, and abandonment to the will of our sovereign King. The soul no longer hesitates but becomes "obsessed with serving the Lord not just a little but as much as it can."

These powerful effects are not present in feigned raptures, which are more like fainting spells or convulsions and are due to a weak constitution. Women are more prone to false raptures, Teresa notes, "for everything seems to us to be an ecstasy." As early as the *Life*, Teresa speaks of the danger of false absorption and attributes it to rabies! In *The Interior Castle*, she ridicules the false experience with a rhyming pun difficult to translate into English. In Spanish the word for rapture is *arrobamiento*. Teresa calls false rapture *abobamiento*, which means foolishness.

Teresa is so concerned about the danger here that she devotes all of chapter 6 of her *Foundations* to the most vehement precautions and urges us to read this over many times. She refers to false rapture as stupefaction, listlessness, or a daze and sees absolutely no value in it because it wastes precious time and wears down our health.

She gives practical advice for stopping false absorption through good food, more sleep, and hard work. We must "get busy with different duties," avoid solitude, and shorten the hours of prayer. We need to let go of our self-will and self-love, submit to spiritual guidance, and trust more in reason because the irrationality of false rapture enslaves the spirit and bogs us down in a quagmire.

We find an excellent description of the prayer of ecstasy in chapter 16 of the *Life*. In these ebullient pages, Teresa is actually experiencing ecstasy as she writes about it. She was not sure how to describe this kind of prayer. On the day she hoped to explain it, God "interrupted" her thanksgiving after Communion and "taught" her how. While she writes, she is "not freed from such holy heavenly madness."

In chapter 17 of the *Life*, the ecstasy has passed and Teresa continues more soberly. Ecstasy is so delightful, we may be tempted to become absorbed in it and may grow lazy and neglect our duties in life. So Teresa carefully explains how the active and contemplative life are joined in this level of prayer. Like Mary sitting at the feet of Jesus (Luke 10:38–42), the will is occupied in its contemplation, without knowing how. But like Martha, busy in the kitchen, the other two faculties can tend to reading, business affairs, and works of charity. Thus Mary and Martha do not work against each other but walk together in harmony.

Meditation

In the following texts, Teresa marvels over the way God delights to be with us as an intimate and understanding companion. Then she makes one of her classic lover's complaints. We see the extent of our intimacy with the very Lord of love in Teresa's meditations on passages from *The Song of Songs* and her comparison with earthly marriage.

As she begins to talk about holy madness, she describes how our Divine Lover brings us into the divine wine cellar to rejoice in his secrets. We are called to be more contemplative like the Blessed Virgin and not overly rational like imbalanced theologians or "learned men."

In her discussion of raptures, Teresa explains what happens to the body and some of the effects of the experience, including radical detachment and a desire for suffering. Highly suspicious of false absorption in ecstasy, she then praises the value of reason.

Her letters to María de San José and Gracián give strong

recommendations for how to treat Isabel de San Jerónimo, an unstable person who thinks she is experiencing mystical ecstasy when she is merely deceived and carried away by her own wild imagination, weeping, talking indiscreetly, and writing down every little feeling.

The final quotations give a good description of perfect contemplation and our call to live a life of action and contemplation, with Martha and Mary in balance.

Teresian Texts: Intimacy and Ecstasy

O my Hope, my Father, my Creator, and my true Lord and Brother! When I consider how You say that Your delights are with the children of men, my soul rejoices greatly. O Lord of heaven and earth, what words these are that no sinner might be wanting in trust! Are You, Lord, perhaps lacking someone with whom to delight that You seek such a foul-smelling little worm like myself?... Oh, what extraordinary mercy and what favor so beyond our ability to deserve! And that mortals forget all of this!... Well, what need is there for my love? Why do You want it, my God, or what do You gain? Oh, may You be blessed! May You be blessed, my God, forever!

(S 7.1–2)

Oh, my Lord, my Mercy, and my Good! And what greater good could I want in this life than to be so close to You, that there be no division between You and me? With this companionship, what can be difficult? What can one not undertake for You, being so closely joined?

(SS 4.9)

God and the soul understand each other.... It's like the experience of two persons here on earth who love each other deeply and understand each other well; even without signs, just by a glance, it seems, they understand each other.... [T]hese two lovers gaze directly at each other, as the Bridegroom says to the Bride in the *Song of Songs.*

(*L* 27.10)

Indeed, I took delight in the Lord today and dared to complain of His Majesty, and I said to Him: "How is it, my God, that it's not enough that You keep me in this miserable life and that for love of You I undergo it and desire to live where everything hinders the enjoyment of You, in that I have to eat and sleep and carry on business and talk with everyone (and I suffer all for love of You, as You well know, my Lord, because it's the greatest torment for me); how is it that when there is so little time left over to enjoy Your presence You hide from me? How is this compatible with Your mercy? How can the love You bear me allow this? I believe, Lord, that if it were possible for me to hide from You as it is for You to hide from me that the love You have for me would not suffer it; but You are with me and see me always. Don't tolerate this, my Lord! I implore You to see that it is injurious to one who loves You so much.... But sometimes love becomes so foolish I don't make sense; with my whole mind I make these complaints, and the Lord puts up with it all.

(*L* 37.8–9)

❖

O my Jesus, who could explain the benefit that lies in throwing ourselves into the arms of this Lord of ours and making an agreement with His Majesty that *I look at my Beloved, and my Beloved at me.*

(*SS* 4.8)

My Lord, I do not ask you for anything else in life but that *You kiss me with the kiss of your mouth,* and that you do so in such a way that although I may want to withdraw from this friendship and union, my will may always, Lord of my life, be subject to Your will and not depart from it; that there will be nothing to impede me from being able to say: "My God and my

Glory, indeed *Your breasts are better and more delightful than wine.*"

(*SS* 3.15)

God espouses souls spiritually.... [E]ven though the comparison may be a coarse one I cannot find another that would better explain what I mean than the sacrament of marriage. This spiritual espousal is different in kind from marriage, for in these matters that we are dealing with there is never anything that is not spiritual. Corporal things are far distant from them, and the spiritual joys the Lord gives when compared with the delights married people must experience are a thousand leagues distant.

(*IC* 5.4.3)

In this state there is no more thought of the body than if the soul were not in it, but one's thought is only of the spirit. In the spiritual marriage, there is still much less remembrance of the body because this secret union takes place in the very interior center of the soul, which must be where God Himself is.

(*IC* 7.2.3)

The spiritual betrothal is different, for the two often separate. ... [T]he favor of union with the Lord passes quickly, and afterward the soul remains without that company; I mean, without awareness of it. In this other favor from the Lord, no. The soul always remains with its God in that center. Let us say that the union is like the joining of two wax candles to such an extent that the flame coming from them is but one, or that the wick, the flame, and the wax are all one. But afterward one candle can be easily separated from the other and there are two candles; the same holds for the wick. In the spiritual marriage the union is like what we have when rain falls from the sky into a river or fount; all is water, for the rain that fell from heaven cannot be divided or separated from the water of the river. Or it is like what we have when a little stream enters the sea, there is no means of separating the two. Or, like the bright light entering a room through two different windows; although the streams of light are separate when entering the room, they become one.

(IC 7.2.4)

❖

A greater or lesser amount can be given a person to drink, a good or a better wine, and the wine will leave him more or less inebriated and intoxicated. So with the favors of the Lord; to one He gives a little wine of devotion, to another more, with another He increases it in such a way that the person begins to go out from himself, from his sensuality, and from all earthly things; to some He gives great fervor in His service; to others, impulses of love; to others, great charity toward their neighbors. These gifts are given in such a way that these persons go about so stupefied they do not feel the great trials that take place here. But much is contained in what the bride says. He brings her into the wine cellar so that she may come out more abundantly enriched. It doesn't seem the King wants to keep anything from her. He wants her to drink in conformity with her desire and become wholly inebriated, drinking of all the wines in God's storehouse. Let the soul rejoice in these joys. Let it admire God's grandeurs. Let it not fear to lose its life from drinking so much beyond what its natural weakness can endure. Let it die in this paradise of delights. Blessed be such a death that so makes one live!

(SS 6.3)

The blessing is the greatest that can be tasted in this life, even if all the delights and pleasures of the world were joined together. ...Let worldly people worry about their lordships, riches, delights, honors, and food, for even if a person were able to enjoy all these things without the accompanying trials — which is impossible — he would not attain in a thousand years the happiness that in one moment is enjoyed by a soul brought here by the Lord.

(SS 4.4.7)

Oh, secrets of God! Here there is no more to do than surrender our intellects and reflect that they are of no avail when it comes to understanding the grandeurs of God. It is good to recall here how God acted with the Blessed Virgin, our Lady. In spite of all her wisdom she asked the angel: *How can this be?* But after he answered, *The Holy Spirit will come upon you; the power of the Most High will overshadow you,* she engaged in no further discussion. As one who had such great faith and wisdom, she understood at once that if these two intervened, there was nothing more to know or doubt. She did not act as do some learned men (whom the Lord does not lead by this mode of prayer and who haven't begun a life of prayer), for they want to be so rational about things and so precise in their understanding that it doesn't seem anyone else but they with their learning can understand the grandeurs of God. If only they would learn something from the humility of the most Blessed Virgin!

(*SS* 6.7)

❖

Rapture and suspension, in my opinion, are both the same. But I am used to saying suspension in order to avoid saying rapture, a word that frightens. And indeed the union just described can also be called suspension. The difference between rapture and union is this: the rapture lasts longer and is felt more exteriorly, for your breathing diminishes in such a way that you are unable to speak or open your eyes. Although this diminishing of these bodily powers occurs in union, it takes place in this prayer with greater force, because the natural heat leaves the body, going I don't know where. When the rapture is intense (for in all these kinds of prayer there is a more and a less), when it is greater, as I say, the hands are frozen and sometimes stretched out like sticks, and the body remains as it is, either standing or kneeling. And the soul is so occupied with rejoicing in what the Lord represents to it that it seemingly forgets to animate the body and leaves the body abandoned; and if the suspension lasts, the nerves are left aching.

(*T* 59.7)

With the speed of a ball shot from an arquebus, when fire is applied, an interior flight is experienced — I don't know what else to call it — which, though noiseless, is so clearly a movement that it cannot be the work of the imagination. And while the spirit is far outside itself, from all it can understand, great things are shown to it. When it again senses that it is within itself, the benefits it feels are remarkable, and it has so little esteem for all earthly things in comparison to the things it has seen that the former seem like dung. From then on its life on earth is very painful, and it doesn't see anything good in those things that used to seem good to it.

(IC 6.5.9)

Oh, when the soul returns completely to itself, what bewilderment and how intense its desires to be occupied in God in every kind of way He might want!... The soul would desire to have a thousand lives so as to employ them all for God and that everything here on earth would be a tongue to help it praise Him.... [T]hese souls complain to His Majesty when no opportunity for suffering presents itself.

(IC 6.4.15)

Enjoyment in prayer is not so habitual that there is not time for everything. I would be suspicious of anyone who says this delight is continual.... Strive to free yourselves from this error and avoid such absorption with all your strength.... For if this absorption continues, it is extremely dangerous at least for the brain and the head.

(IC 6.7.13)

Anything that so controls us that we know our reason is not free should be held as suspect. Know that liberty of spirit will never be gained in this way. For one of the traits reason has is that it can find God in all things and be able to think about them. All the rest is subjection of spirit and, apart from the harm done to the body, so binds the soul as to hinder growth. The soul here resembles someone on a journey who enters a quagmire or swamp and thus cannot move onward. And, in order to advance, a soul must not only walk but fly. This immobility happens frequently when, as they say (and it seems to them), they are immersed in the divinity and cannot help themselves or find a remedy by diverting their attention because they are suspended.

(F 6.15)

❖

I wish I were equally sure about San Jerónimo. I am really worried about that woman. Believe me, she ought either never to have left me or she should have gone where there was somebody she was afraid of. Please God the devil may not play some trick with her, or we shall have our hands full. Your Reverence should instruct the Prioress not to let her write another word, and, until she gets a letter from me, she herself must be told that I realize she is in the grip of a very evil humor, or, if not of that, of something worse.... San Jerónimo said nothing about such things (when she was) here, because the Prioress used to cut her short at once, and reprove her, so she kept quiet; when I was at Seville, as you saw, she used not to get very far with the subject either. I don't know if we made a mistake in allowing her to leave us. Please God all may be well.

Think what a business it would have been if the paper which the Prioress found had been discovered by the other nuns. God forgive whoever told her to write it. Our Father would like me to write to her severely on the matter. Read the enclosed letter which I have written her, and send it her if you think it is all right. You are acting very wisely indeed in not allowing them to speak to anyone.... It must be very trying to have her going about among the other nuns weeping like that and for them to be seeing her continually writing. Get hold of whatever it is she writes and send it to me, and take away the illusion she has that she is going to be allowed to talk about it to anybody but our Father: it is talking to people about it that has been so bad for her.

(Le 172–73 to María de San José)

Before I forget: I do not approve of your nuns' writing on subjects to do with prayer; there are many disadvantages in the practice which I should like to mention. You must realize that it is not only a waste of time; it interferes with the soul's freedom of action; and then, too, it may lead the nuns to imagine all kinds of things. If I remember, I will say this to our Father; if I do not, you should speak to him about it yourself. If their experiences are of any substance, they will never forget them; and if they are of a kind that can be forgotten, there is no point in their writing them down. It will be sufficient if they tell our Father what they remember of them when they see him. It seems to me they are quite safe if they do that, and, if there is one thing which can do them harm, it is attributing importance to things they see or hear.... If I had appeared to attach any importance to the things San Jerónimo told me, she would never have stopped, so I said nothing, though actually I thought some of them were genuine. Believe me, the best thing for the nuns to do is to praise the Lord Who gives these things, and, as soon as they are over, just let them be: what matters is the profit they bring the soul....

I was extremely glad to hear that our Father is telling those two nuns who are so much given to prayer that they must eat meat. You know, my daughter, I have been worried about them: they would not have had such a whirl of experiences if they had been with me. The very fact that they have so many of these experiences makes me suspicious about them, and, though some of them may be genuine, I am sure it will be best if they regard them as of little importance, and if your Reverence and our Father do the same, or indeed treat them as of no account at all, for nothing will be lost by that even if they are genuine. By making no account of them I mean you should say that God leads some souls by one road and some by another, and that this particular road is not one that leads to the greatest sanctity, which is quite true.

(*Le* 223 and 233 to María de San José)

As for (Isabel de) San Jerónimo, she will have to be made to eat meat for a few days, and to give up prayer, and your Paternity must order her to have no communication with anyone but yourself, or, in writing, with me. For she has an unsteady imagination which leads her to think she is seeing and hearing the things she meditates upon. At the same time, she may occasionally be right, as she has sometimes been in the past, for she is a very good soul.

The same, I think, is true of Beatriz, though what they tell me happened at the time of her profession seems to be no fancy but a wonderful favor. She must fast very little. Tell the Prioress not to allow them to be at prayer all the time, but to keep them busy with other offices, lest we find worse things happening. Believe me, this is really necessary.

(*Le* 122 to Gracián)

✤

If a person is reflecting upon some scriptural event, it becomes as lost to the memory as it would be if there had never been any thought of it. If the person reads, there is no remembrance of what he read; nor is there any remembrance if he prays vocally. Thus this bothersome little moth, which is the memory, gets its wings burnt here; it can no longer move. The will is fully occupied in loving, but it doesn't understand how it loves. The intellect, if it understands, doesn't understand how it understands; at least it can't comprehend anything of what it understands. It doesn't seem to me that it understands, because, as I say, it doesn't understand—I really can't understand this!

(*L* 18.14)

In the prayer of quiet the soul didn't desire to move or stir, rejoicing in that holy idleness of Mary; and in this prayer it can also be Martha in such a way that it is as though engaged in both the active and contemplative life together. It tends to works of charity and to business affairs that have to do with its state in life and to reading; although it isn't master of itself completely. And it understands clearly that the best part of the soul is somewhere else. It's as though we were speaking to someone at our side and from the other side another person were speaking to us; we wouldn't be fully attentive to either the one or the other. This prayer is something that is felt very clearly, and it gives deep satisfaction and happiness when it is experienced. It is an excellent preparation so that the soul may reach a profound quiet when it has time for solitude, or leisure from business matters.

(*L* 17.4)

Chapter 8

The "Spooky Stuff"

Perfection as well as its reward does not consist in spiritual delights but in greater love and in deeds done with greater justice and truth.
(IC 3.2.10)

We come now to Teresa's extraordinary mystical experiences — visions, locutions, revelations, raptures, transports. Some refer to these as her "spooky stuff." Teresa called these "favors" or "spiritual delights," and indeed they are. But her language can be misleading and give these experiences more merit than they deserve. Classic mystical theology calls these experiences "secondary psychophysical phenomena." This terminology is more awkward than that used by Teresa, but, for several reasons, it is far more accurate.

These experiences — in their external Teresian form — are not essential but accidental, not primary but secondary, not spiritual but psychic and physical, as the classic term implies. Psychophysical phenomena have only limited value, if any. They are the result of an inner experience projected outward. This outer manifestation depends on temperament, predisposition, and spiritual maturity, even on the culture and era in which we live. It also depends on whether we are "transparent" or "opaque."

The opaque personality sees the same comedy as the transparent but never laughs; hears the same music but never moves a muscle; suffers the same embarrassment but never turns red. The inner experience of the transparent personality, however, always registers externally. What happens in the depths rises easily to the surface and somehow is manifested outwardly. What happens in the deep recesses of the opaque personality seldom, if ever, becomes apparent. Transparent personalities are far more likely to translate their inner experience into painting, poetry, or song. If they are spiritual, they are likely to translate their inner experience of God into visions, locutions, and raptures, as the transparent Teresa did.

Both the transparent and opaque person truly experience union with God, but only the transparent one is conscious of it. Both are drawn by God into the mystical depths, but only the transparent exhibits the secondary psychophysical phenomena. Both types, however, may be holy. The opaque person may in fact be holier. As Teresa points out, the holiest are not those who experience "favors" but those who exhibit the greatest virtue, service, and purity of conscience. She goes even further and explains that God sometimes grants these "favors" to those "in a bad state" in order to get their attention and convert them. She herself was one of these sleepers who desperately needed to wake up.

Theologically, both transparent and opaque persons are mystics. But phenomenally, only the former are because they *express* their inner experience of God and are *recognizably* mystical. In this sense, mysticism is loving, experiential *awareness* of God.

The mystic is not a special kind of person, as we see from the normalcy of Teresa's life. But every person is a special kind of mystic. Teresa was a woman and not a man, was Spanish and not Japanese, was of the sixteenth and not the twentieth century. In other words, Teresa was Teresa and not someone else. Though all of us share a common ground essential to the inner experience of God, we do not share accidental features of that experience. We make a serious mistake when we look at the highly particularized form of Teresa's mystical experience and universalize it. This leads us to an even more serious mistake: We admire her experience and want to imitate it.

When Teresa first began to experience these phenomena, she was confused and frightened. She didn't understand what was happening and couldn't find anyone to help her. When she finally talked to St. Peter Alcántara and others who assured her, she calmed down, but was still characteristically enthused about these phenomena. As she matured, however, she became far more cautious and even minimized these experiences as she wrote and counselled others. She knew that if we are too predisposed to them, we are likely to be deceived.

There is yet another reason to minimize these secondary psychophysical phenomena. When we first begin to recognize our experience of God, we are neophytes and unused to it. Our psychophysical makeup is too weak and our capacity too small to bear the experience. So the effects on the body are overwhelming, as Teresa so aptly describes. We feel like a piece of straw picked up by a mighty giant or a tiny boat tossed about on a storm-swept sea.

As we grow deeper and more spiritual, however, our psychophysical organism grows stronger, and our capacity to bear the experience of God increases. Since we become more accommodated to the inner experience, the intensity of secondary phenomena decreases. We see this clearly in Teresa as she grows from the near hysteria of her first experiences depicted in the *Life* to the mature capacity and calm she enjoyed in the later years of her life, when these phenomena almost disappeared.

There is another problem with Teresa's early descriptions of her mystical experiences. She limits herself too much to formal, circumscribed moments. By using such formal and even formidable terms as "locution," "vision," and "transport," Teresa inadvertently skews what should be understood as a natural part of the ebb and flow of life. When she describes "flight of the spirit," it makes us look self-consciously for some clearly circumscribed event to occur in our lives, when in fact we are often "carried away" by our experience of God. Teresa's language makes us look for *a* rapture and perhaps miss the inevitable enrapturing that occurs regularly throughout the day. To speak in terms of visions and locutions is to forget how normal it should be to "hear" and "see" the God who, being madly in love with us, longs to communicate with us and make the divine presence felt, if only we have eyes to see and ears to hear. And of course loving hurts us. We need not distract ourselves looking for some particular, circumscribed "wound of love."

This approach in no way reduces the heights of Teresa's mysticism to the merely natural level. Instead, it shows the inevitable convergence of the natural and supernatural. More importantly, it makes Teresa's seemingly rarified and reified mystical experience more accessible to us and more a part of our ordinary human experience. Surely this is how Teresa understood it and how God intended it to be. With all this clarification in mind, we are now ready to look at the "spooky stuff."

Visions

Teresa describes three types of visions. One is called *imaginary*, not because it is pure fantasy but because it takes the form of a visual image that is seen with the "eyes of the soul." The *intellectual* vision is a sudden, nonrepresentational awareness. A *corporeal* vision is perceived with the eyes of the body. All of Teresa's visions were of the first two types. She never had a corporeal vision. She experienced visions frequently for two and a half years in her early forties. Then they ceased and were replaced by a more sublime and advanced prayer: impulses of love.

What did Teresa "see" in her visions? She saw many of those she loved in heaven: her parents, her favorite confessors, several Jesuits whom she revered. She saw the Blessed Trinity and the Holy Spirit with wings made of tiny tinkling shells. After the founding of St. Joseph's in Avila, Mary and Joseph vested her in a white robe of shining brightness and placed a golden necklace around her throat. Christ placed a crown on her head and thanked her for what she did to honor his mother.

There is something charmingly "Teresian" about Teresa's visions of Christ. Because of our natural human weakness, we cannot bear the full reality of God all at once. So Christ in his infinite goodness revealed himself to Teresa little by little. She first saw his hands and could not get over their magnificence: "The beauty and the whiteness of one hand alone is completely beyond our imagination." Next she saw his face with all its love, tenderness, and affability. His mouth was not only beautiful but severe. Finally, she was able to see his full sacred humanity in its risen form and exclaimed: "Glorified bodies have such beauty!" She describes the brilliant white light, which surpasses everything imaginable here on earth.

Then Teresa makes a confession — which makes her story irresistible. She admits that she was dying to know how tall Jesus was and the color of his eyes. But because she grasped at this knowledge, she never found out and lost the vision entirely. We cannot do anything to see more or less, to induce the vision or resist it. When we do, God takes away our power to see what we so greedily desire.

But not all Teresa's visions were consoling. Christ not only comforted her when he made his presence felt; he also often scolded her. At a Mass celebrated by a priest in serious sin, she saw the devil's horns wrapped around the poor man's throat. At the funeral of a wicked person who had died without confessing, Teresa saw a number of devils inside the grave, dragging the body from one to another with large, terrifying hooks. In another vision she saw herself standing alone in a large field, surrounded by enemies with daggers, swords, and long rapiers.

Teresa describes what happens in a vision, especially an intellectual one, which is fundamentally an experience of *presence.* She makes a strong distinction between a true vision, which is rare, and the more common experience of presence many of us enjoy in the lower levels of prayer.

A genuine vision has several distinct characteristics:

1. It is *gratuitous,* which means that it is beyond our control, and nothing we do can bring it about.

2. It is *sudden* and *unexpected,* not subject to our beck and call. It seldom occurs during contemplation. In other words, God's self-revelation is usually not offered to a person *at* prayer, but to a person *of* prayer.

3. It is *brief* and passes quickly, like a streak of lightning, if it is imaginative. An intellectual vision, however, being formless and therefore more interior, can last many days and sometimes even more than a year.

4. It is *certain*. Though there may be an initial healthy caution and fear of delusion, eventually doubt has no force.

5. It is *enlightening*. Without any effort to study or learn, one is instantly knowledgeable and wise.

6. It is *hidden*. The true visionary is utterly discreet, reveals his or her secret only to the appropriate persons, and would rather die a thousand deaths than have these experiences publicly known.

7. It is *not sought after* and in fact is strongly *resisted*.

8. Its *effects* are *extraordinary*. The person who experiences visions does not continue to live an ordinary, mediocre life. The true visionary becomes enflamed with extraordinary virtue, especially humility and obedience, and lives a life of *heroic* service and suffering.

It is illuminating to contrast these signs with the characteristics of spurious visions today. Contemporary false visionaries betray their inauthenticity by having their visions "on call," at a regularly scheduled time and place, often in public, among adoring and credulous devotees. They enjoy the public acclaim and go on the lecture circuit talking about their experiences and even "performing" them on stage — for pay! Their lives remain ordinary, comfortable, and bourgeois — with a pious veneer; or they often become notorious — sexually or financially.

This should be kept in mind when one evaluates the charismatic movement's so-called gifts of tongues or healing, the New Age channeler's staged or published disclosures, or the pietistic housewife's visions of Mary that turn her rosary gold, give her the scent of roses, and lead her to proclaim "messages" of what we must do if the ultimate cosmic cataclysm is not to befall the planet.

Many of us are so repulsed by the inauthentic mystical experience rampant today, we find it difficult to respond positively to Teresa. We need to make more of an effort to be open to her tested and authenticated experience.

Locutions

Teresa describes three kinds of locutions: those that are explicit and heard with our bodily sense of hearing, those that are explicit and communicated silently through inner voices, and those that are not at all explicit.

Teresa often experienced these "voices" in great variety. Some were comforting and made her "dissolve in love." Some were words of rebuke and made her tremble. Some reminded her of her past sins, advised her about her present course of action, or warned her of future trouble for herself or others.

There is tremendous danger of illusion here, so in both the *Life* and *The Interior Castle*, Teresa clearly distinguishes between a genuine locution from God and one that is self-induced, fabricated by the imagination, or merely the familiar voice of conscience.

The genuine locution is "heard" and not composed. Even when we are agitated, we don't lose a single syllable. It is clear and certain, not indistinct, muffled, or "half-dreamed." It comes suddenly and unexpectedly, sometimes even during our conversations. It is not at all within our power and can't be called up on schedule — or ignored. The genuine locution is never mere words but actually effects what the words say. If we are afraid, and the words say "fear not," we are left calm and free of distress.

A genuine locution leaves a person *radically* changed. It results in light, quiet, and peace, not confusion, agitation, and fear; true and not false humility; proper fear of delusion; obedience to spiritual guidance, not overconfident self-validation. In a genuine locution we often hear what we don't want to: painful words of criticism, rebuke, and reprimand. In the self-induced false locution, we hear only what we want to hear: words that either comfort or make us feel falsely superior to others because of our "secret knowledge." The false locution is often the mere projection of our own unexpressed desires.

Teresa claims that discernment is relatively easy if we are experienced and "on the lookout." Persons of experience will rarely be deceived unless they choose to be. The problem today is a tragic lack of experienced spiritual leaders. Those who learn these signs of authenticity can mistakenly believe in their own visions and voices without any malicious intent to deceive. And the typical spiritual director, parish priest, prayer group, psychotherapist, or gullible audience is fooled — simply because the "mystic" is a "good person" and well intentioned.

Teresa was almost ruthless in her evaluation of mystical experiences — especially in her later years. She advocated "great care" in this area. "For in regard to these fancies," she said, "things have been told to me that have left me amazed at how it is possible for such persons truly to think that they see (or hear) what they do not."

Teresa was often asked to discern the authenticity of mystical phenomena. She used her common sense and was not afraid to call these experiences absurdities, nonsense, or "just wild talk." She was fully aware that trancelike states are not always genuinely spiritual but may arise from purely pathological causes, from obsessive mental concentration, or from the emotional and aesthetic impact of music, poetry, art, or nature. Today we are too ignorant, too credulous, or too cowardly to make the value judgments Teresa did and "test the spirits." How we need the likes of her today!

Ignoring Secondary Phenomena

When we understand the true nature of secondary psychophysical phenomena and see how cautious even Teresa is — though she is not as cautious as St. John of the Cross — we can appreciate the classic Carmelite approach to these experiences. Since it is so easy to be deluded or even to cling to such consolations, we must resist and ignore them. Under no circumstances are we to ask for them. If we do not treat them with lighthearted detachment, they can, and often do, become serious impediments to spiritual growth.

Teresa tells us she asked for spiritual delight only once in her life. When she realized what she was doing, she became very annoyed with herself. She fills her writings, then, with compelling reasons why we should never desire favors. In chapter 2 of the Fourth Mansion and again in chapter 9 of the Sixth, she explains how such a request sets us up to be deceived. We show lack of trust and humility and presumptuously think we can bear the sufferings these favors entail. She uses the example of John of the Cross, who begged God *not* to give him delights because he wanted to serve his Lord for love and not for "pay."

As Teresa teaches, love of God and union do not consist in spiritual consolations but in humility, fortitude, heroic deeds, and faithful service. We must not advise God about what should be given to us; rather, we must conform our will to the divine will. This is not merely one practice at the beginning of the spiritual journey, but the greatest perfection attainable every step of the way.

God alone knows what is fitting for us. There are no certain rules, for God gives when, how, and to whom he desires, leading us along many different paths suited to our unique individuality: "Perhaps the one who thinks she is walking along a very lowly path is in fact higher in the eyes of the Lord."

God is lavish and ends up giving far more than we desire. But we must never think that we "deserve" something, based on the time we have put in and the services we have rendered. We must give up counting altogether and count instead on God's good graces. Comparisons with others are insidious. What does it matter if God gives to another after a few days what hasn't been granted to me after many years? All we can do is wait. Can a toad fly whenever it wants? Neither can our spirit. So "let us leave it to the Lord" and prepare ourselves by drinking the chalice of suffering.

Meditation

In the following texts, Teresa describes some of her visions (at first using the third person) and distinguishes a genuine vision from the sense of presence we normally experience in ordinary levels of prayer. Then she describes the signs of a genuine locution and urges us to be cautious around those with melancholy personalities and weak (unstable) imaginations.

As Teresa astutely advises us to ignore secondary psychophysical phenomena, she reminds us that we deserve nothing, despite our generous service and good behavior. We must be humble enough to trust God to give us what we most need.

In her letter to her brother Lorenzo, written in January 1577 from Toledo, Teresa explains how ashamed she feels because she has temporarily begun to experience raptures again. She sounds as if she's reporting the recurrence of some troublesome disease, and she prays to be delivered from them, for they do not improve her prayer. Then she tells Lorenzo how to respond to his own experience of secondary psychophysical phenomena: He must ignore both his joy and his evil feelings and pay no attention to either the body's tremblings or its heat, for these add no value to his spiritual life and will soon disappear as he grows deeper and stronger.

Teresian Texts: The "Spooky Stuff"

It seemed to her that He was always looking at her. . . . She felt He was so near that He couldn't fail to hear her. But she didn't hear words spoken whenever she wanted; only unexpectedly when they were necessary. She felt He was walking at her right side, but she didn't experience this with those senses by which we can know that a person is beside us. This vision comes in another unexplainable, more delicate way. . . . In the visions that come through the senses one can be deceived, but not in the intellectual vision.

(*IC* 6.8.3)

While the soul is very far from thinking that anything will be seen, or having the thought even pass through its mind, suddenly the vision is represented to it all at once and stirs all the faculties and senses with a great fear and tumult so as to place them afterward in that happy peace. Just as there was a tempest and tumult that came from heaven when St. Paul was hurled to the ground, here in this interior world there is a great stirring; and in a moment, as I have said, all remains calm, and this soul is left so well instructed.

(*IC* 6.9.10)

Being in prayer on the feastday of the glorious St. Peter, I saw or, to put it better, I felt Christ beside me; I saw nothing with my bodily eyes or with my soul, but it seemed to me that Christ was at my side — I saw that it was He, in my opinion, Who was speaking to me. Since I was completely unaware that there could be a vision like this one, it greatly frightened me in the beginning; I did nothing but weep. However, by speaking one word alone to assure me, the Lord left me feeling as I usually did: quiet, favored, and without any fear. It seemed to me that Jesus Christ was always present at my side; but since this wasn't an imaginative vision, I didn't see any form. Yet I felt very clearly that He was always present at my right side and that He was the witness of everything I did. At no time in which I was a little recollected, or not greatly distracted, was I able to ignore that He was present at my side.

(*L* 27.2)

This vision is not like the presence of God that is often felt, especially by those who experience the prayer of union or quiet, in which it seems that in desiring to begin to practice prayer we find Him to speak to, and it seems we know that He hears us through the effects and spiritual feelings of great love and faith that we tenderly experience, and through other resolutions. This presence is a great favor from God and should be highly esteemed by the one He gives it to, for it is a very sublime prayer, but it is not a vision; in this prayer of union or quiet one understands that God is present by the effects that, as I say, He grants to the soul — that is the way His Majesty wants to give the experience of Himself. In this vision it is seen clearly that Jesus Christ, son of the Virgin, is present. In the prayer of union or quiet some impressions of the Divinity are bestowed; in this vision, along with the impressions, you see that also the most sacred humanity accompanies us and desires to grant us favors.

(L 27.4)

It is a light so different from earthly light that the sun's brightness that we see appears very tarnished in comparison with that brightness and light represented to the sight, and so different that afterward you wouldn't want to open your eyes. It's like the difference between a sparkling, clear water that flows over crystal and which the sun is reflecting and a very cloudy, muddy water flowing along the ground. This doesn't mean that the sun is represented or that the light resembles sunlight. It seems in fact like natural light, and the sunlight seems artificial. It is a light that has no night; nothing troubles it. In sum, it is of such a kind that a person couldn't imagine what it is like in all the days of his life no matter how powerful the intellect.

(L 28.5)

The Lord almost always showed Himself to me as risen, also when He appeared in the Host — except at times when He showed me His wounds in order to encourage me when I was suffering tribulation. Sometimes He appeared on the cross or in the garden, and a few times with the crown of thorns; sometimes He also appeared carrying the cross on account, as I say, of my needs and those of others. But His body was always glorified.

(L 29.4)

❖

The more it hears words of favor the more humble it should be left; if it isn't, let it believe that the spirit is not from God. One thing very certain is that when the spirit is from God the soul esteems itself less, the greater the favor granted, and it has more awareness of its sins and is more forgetful of its own gain, and its will and memory are employed more in seeking only the honor of God,...and it walks with greater fear lest its will deviate in anything.

(*IC* 6.3.17)

Sometimes, and often, the locution can be an illusion, especially in persons with a weak [unstable] imagination or in those who are melancholic, I mean who suffer noticeably from melancholy.

In my opinion, no attention should be paid to these latter two kinds of persons even if they say they see and hear and understand. But neither should one disturb these persons by telling them their locutions come from the devil; one must listen to them as to sick persons. The prioress or confessor to whom they relate their locutions should tell them to pay no attention to such experiences, that these locutions are not essential to the service of God, and that the devil has deceived many by such means, even though this particular person, perhaps, may not be suffering such deception. This counsel should be given so as not to aggravate the melancholy, for if they tell her the locution is due to melancholy, there will be no end to the matter; she will swear that she sees and hears, for it seems to her that she does.

(*IC* 6.3.1–2)

For both the sick and the healthy there is always reason to fear these things until the spirit of such persons is well understood. And I say that in the beginning it is always better to free these persons from such experiences, for if the locutions are from God, doing so is a greater help toward progress, and a person even grows when tested. This is true; nonetheless, one should not proceed in a way that is distressing or disturbing to a soul, because truly the soul can't help it if these locutions come.

(*IC* 6.3.3)

✤

It is dangerous to count the number of years in which you have practiced prayer; even though humility may be present, I think there can remain a kind of feeling that you deserve something for the service.... [A]ny spiritual person who thinks that he deserves these delights of spirit for the many years he has practiced prayer will not ascend to the summit of the spiritual life.... [T]hose years of service should be forgotten; for in comparison with one drop of the blood the Lord shed for us, everything we do is disgusting.

(L 39.15–16)

These are gifts God gives when He desires and how He desires, and they depend neither on time nor on services. I do not mean that time and services are not important, but often the contemplation the Lord doesn't give to one in twenty years He gives to another in one. His Majesty knows the reason.

(L 34.11)

You have no reason to be afflicted.... [T]rust in His goodness who never fails His friends. Conceal from your eyes the thought about why He gives devotion to one after such a few days and not to me after so many years. Let us believe that all is for our own greater good. Let His Majesty lead the way along the path He desires. We belong no longer to ourselves but to Him.

(L 11.12)

Humility! humility! By this means the Lord allows Himself to be conquered with regard to anything we want from Him. The first sign for seeing whether or not you have humility is that you do not think you deserve these favors and spiritual delights from the Lord or that you will receive them in your lifetime.

(IC 4.2.9)

Sometimes God leads the weakest along this path. And so there is nothing in it to approve or condemn. One should consider the virtues and who it is who serves our Lord with greater mortification, humility, and purity of conscience; this is the one who will be the holiest.... In heaven we will be surprised to see how different His judgment is from what we can understand here below.

(*IC* 6.8.10)

Oh, when God so wills, how He is revealed openly without these little helps from us! For however much we may do, He carries off the spirit as a giant would a piece of straw — and no resistance suffices. What a strange belief it is, that the toad should expect to fly of itself whenever it wants. And it seems to me to be even more difficult and troublesome for our spirit to raise itself up if God doesn't raise it, for it is weighed down with the earth and a thousand obstacles, and wanting to fly profits it little. Although flying is more natural to it than to the toad, it is so bogged down in the mud that through its own fault it lost this ability.

(*L* 22.13)

Let us leave it to the Lord. (For He knows us better than we do ourselves. And true humility is content with what is received.) There are some persons who demand favors from God as though these were due them in justice. That's a nice kind of humility! Thus, He who knows all very seldom grants such persons favors, and rightly so. He sees clearly that they are not ready to drink from the chalice.

(*W* 18.6)

His Majesty knows best what is suitable for us. There's no need for us to be advising Him about what He should give us, for He can rightly tell us that we don't know what we're asking for. The whole aim of any person who is beginning prayer — and don't forget this, because it's very important — should be that he work and prepare himself with determination and every possible effort to bring his will into conformity with God's will. Be certain that, as I shall say later, the greatest perfection attainable along the spiritual path lies in this conformity. It is the person who lives in more perfect conformity who will receive more from the Lord and be more advanced on this road. Don't think that in what concerns perfection there is some mystery or things unknown or things to be still understood, for in perfect conformity to God's will lies all our good.

(*IC* 2.1.8)

❖

I must tell you that, for over a week, I have been in such a condition that, if it were to go on, I should hardly be able to attend to all my business. Since before I wrote to you I have had raptures again, and they have been most distressing. Several times I have had them in public — during Matins, for example. It is useless to resist them and they are impossible to conceal. I get so dreadfully ashamed that I feel I want to hide away somewhere. I pray God earnestly not to let them happen to me in public: will you make this prayer for me too, for it is an extremely awkward thing and I don't believe my prayer is any the better for it? Latterly I have been going about almost as if I were drunk; but at least it is clear that the soul is well employed. . . .

Pay no attention to those evil feelings which come to you afterwards. I have never suffered from them myself, since God, of His goodness, has always delivered me from such passions, but I think the explanation of them must be that the soul's joy is so keen that it makes itself felt in the body. With God's help it will calm down if you take no notice of it. Several people have discussed this with me.

Those trembling fits will stop too. As the experience is a new one the soul takes fright, and with good reason; but after several repetitions it will become used to receiving favors. Resist the trembling fits, and any other outward manifestations, as far as you can, or they may become habitual, and that would be more of a hindrance than a help.

This heat which you say you experience will neither help nor hinder [your prayer], but it might well do some harm to your health, if it occurred often. It may perhaps gradually stop, like the trembling. These things, as I understand it, have to do with one's constitution: as yours is sanguine, they may be caused by the violent working of the spirit, together with the [body's] natural heat; you concentrate on higher things and [the intensity of your concentration] is felt in the heart. But, as I say, this adds nothing to the value of your prayer.

(*Le* 163 to Lorenzo)

Chapter 9

Signs of Growth

It is necessary that your foundation consist of more than prayer and contemplation. If you do not strive for the virtues and practice them, you will always be dwarfs. And, please God, it will be only a matter of not growing, for you already know that whoever does not increase decreases. I hold that love, where present, cannot possibly be content with remaining always the same.

(*IC* 7.4.9)

We have seen how Teresa describes stages of growth along the royal road in terms of intimacy in marriage, watering a garden, and entering seven mansions of an interior castle. Spiritual betrothal occurs in the Sixth Mansion, which is equivalent to the fourth water Teresa discusses in her *Life*. Spiritual marriage occurs in the Seventh Mansion. In the last chapters of *The Interior Castle*, Teresa gives us a sublime portrait of what awaits us if we, too, are faithful. What does the culmination of the spiritual quest look like?

At this stage of spiritual growth we develop an even higher level of self-awareness. "Knowing ourselves is something so important," Teresa insisted, "that I wouldn't want any relaxation ever in this regard, however high you may have climbed into the heavens. While we are on this earth nothing is more important to us than humility." Because we know ourselves more, even at this advanced level, we fear ourselves more. This is not servile or neurotic fear, but vigilance and healthy caution. We maturely trust ourselves less because we trust God more and surrender the keys of our will so that all our actions conform to the divine will. Therefore we can be tranquil no matter what God gives us:

"If He wants to bring the soul to heaven, it goes, if to hell, it feels no grief since it goes with its God; if its life comes to an end, this it desires; if it lives a thousand years, this too it desires. Let His Majesty treat it as His own — the soul no longer belongs to itself. It is given over entirely to the Lord — it completely overlooks itself."

The Spirit of Freedom

At this level of growth we enjoy a great spirit of freedom and detachment from self in a state Teresa calls "strange forgetfulness." Today we might call it "no-self." The soul — that is, the human person — "goes about so forgetful of self that it thinks it has partly lost its being. In this state everything is directed to the honor of God."

Our attitude toward suffering changes dramatically. Whereas we merely tolerated it earlier, now we actually desire it. "You already know of the espousal between you and Me," Jesus told Teresa. "Because of this espousal, whatever I have is yours. So I give you all the trials and sufferings I underwent." United so intimately with Christ, we can rejoice in persecution without hostile feelings toward those who hurt us. Even though the princess of Eboli tried to destroy Teresa by denouncing her to the Inquisition, Teresa showed her compassion. When the princess was imprisoned for her part in the assassination of a high court official, Teresa sent Gracián to visit her.

At the time of the persecution of the Reform, salacious rumors circulated accusing Gracián of "indecencies" — dancing naked before the Discalced nuns and being the latest in Teresa's long line of lovers. Teresa laughed these off as "nice stories about us" and wrote Salazar: "Personally, I was very little affected by it: nowadays such things leave me completely unmoved." She even called the whole conflict one of God's mercies. Earlier in her life she had written to Pedro Ibañez: "When I go to prayer, no feelings of hostility toward my critics remain in me. For when I first hear about some criticism, it causes me a little feeling of opposition but no disquiet or disturbance. Rather, when I sometimes see other persons taking pity on me, it happens that I laugh to myself; for all the insults in this life seem to be of such little consequence that there is nothing to feel sorry about."

Here in the Seventh Mansion we experience such peace of soul that we no longer fuss about feelings of joy or pain, success or failure, aridity or ecstasy. The experience of rapture is replaced by deep stillness. Our emotional life stabilizes, and we suffer less intensity and fewer extremes. As Teresa said: "It is usually my nature that when I desire something I am impulsive in my desire for it. Now, my desires bear with them such quiet that when I see them fulfilled I don't even know if I rejoice. Sorrow and rejoicing, except in matters of prayer, are completely softened in intensity." We see this growth clearly when we compare Teresa's first and last spiritual testimonies. In 1560 she wrote: "I receive a very intense, consuming impulse for God that I cannot resist. It seems my life is coming to an end, and so this impulse makes me cry out and call to God; and it comes with great frenzy. Sometimes I'm unable to remain seated because of the vomitings from which I suffer." In contrast, twenty years later, she wrote to her dear friend and confessor Dr. Alonso Velázquez: "Oh, who would be able to explain to your Excellency the quiet and calm my soul experiences!... This soul is no longer in part subject to the miseries of the world as it used to be. For although it suffers more, this is only on the surface. The soul is like a lord in his castle, and so it doesn't lose its peace."

Spaciousness and Spontaneity

At this stage our interior being dilates into a vast spaciousness without boundaries or limitations. Teresa returns again to water imagery and describes the human soul as a fountain that doesn't overflow into a stream because its capacity is now infinitely expansive: "The more water there is flowing into it the larger the trough becomes." Teresa speaks glowingly about a "holy freedom" from tension and constraint. We become so "affable, agreeable, and pleasing to persons with whom we deal" that they are not intimidated but attracted to virtue because of our example. The absence of repression and tenseness draws people to us like a magnet. We become like water itself, fluid and spontaneous. So in almost the same breath, Teresa can write to friends about their bad thoughts and aridity in prayer, send a trout or a pot of jam, complain to one about a defective stove, and advise another to avoid the livestock business.

When we reach this level, powerful transforming energy is released. We become so courageous that if we were "cut in pieces for God," we would be greatly consoled. We are consumed with ardent desires to serve — "not just a little," but unto death, like Peter and Paul, two of Teresa's favorite saints. We become "servants of love." Our love for God is not merely fabricated in our imaginations but proven in deeds of heroic proportion.

This brings Teresa again to one of her dominant themes, addressed in each of her major works: the union of the active and the contemplative life. Here Martha and Mary walk together, since "love turns work into rest." At this stage we gladly sacrifice the delights of solitude and prayer in order to serve. The interior calm we now experience is not for our own enjoyment. It fortifies us so that we may endure much less calm in the exterior events of our lives, so that we may have the strength to serve.

At the end of her life, then, Teresa did not move into retirement but more passionately into the thick of the fray. "It would be a great comfort if I could write to you oftener," she told Lorenzo, "but I have so much work to do that I can't. Even tonight [my writing] has kept me from prayer." In a letter to María de San José, she said: "The number of letters I had at Seville is nothing by comparison with what I have had since I came here [to Toledo]: it is really terrible." She later admitted that the worry of "this continual letter-writing" was killing her. In a touching moment only two weeks before her death, she wrote to Catalina de Cristo: "We are on a journey, and, with all the business I have to do, I hardly know where I am."

The tension between Mary and Martha, contemplation and action, prayer and service, is classic and not easily resolved.

Each of us must find the right rhythm, appropriate to our state in life. Teresa struggled her entire lifetime with this issue. How did she resolve it without becoming a workaholic? She devotes all of chapter 5 of the *Foundations* to this crucial question and teaches us to avoid two extremes: the indolence that makes us want to pray when we should work (leading to false absorption) and the sloth that makes us want to work when we should pray (leading to workaholism). "No one can give what he does not have," Teresa insisted. She did not set up a false dichotomy between work and prayer but demanded inspired service enlightened by God, since action without contemplation is blind.

Meditation

In the following texts, Teresa once again emphasizes the importance of self-knowledge even at the highest levels of spiritual growth. She prays with us for the death of the "I" or inflated ego and rejoices in emotional stability and the absence of repression and tension.

The passages from the last pages of *The Interior Castle* summarize the powerful effects of growth in the Seventh Mansion. We have seen these effects all along the royal road in differing degrees of intensity. At this stage, they are remarkably strong and heroic. Note well that we never achieve a permanent state of perfect growth but only a *habitual orientation.*

Teresa dramatically asserts again that spiritual growth is not a matter of consolation and delight but for the sake of laborious service (in imitation of Christ, in the union of both Martha and Mary) and, in particular, for the sake of those nearest to us. Thinking globally is of little value to the planet if we do not act locally, especially within our own families and communities. The greatest spiritual growth does not take us out of this world in isolated, gnostic splendor but moves us profoundly into the gospel ordinariness required in our own little corner of the world.

The series of texts from chapter 5 of the *Foundations* gives us Teresa's wisdom on the tension between work and prayer, distilled from her lifetime of personal struggle with this issue. The final passage is Teresa's most sublime poem, describing the reconciliation of opposites in the highest reaches of the Seventh Mansion where struggle becomes triumph, labor becomes rest, and sorrowing becomes serenity.

Teresian Texts: Signs of Growth

This path of self knowledge must never be abandoned, nor is there on this journey a soul so much a giant that it has no need to return often to the stage of an infant and suckling. And this should never be forgotten. Perhaps I shall speak of it more often because it is very important. There is no stage of prayer so sublime that it isn't necessary to return often to the beginning. Along this path of prayer, self knowledge and the thought of one's sins is the bread with which all palates must be fed no matter how delicate they may be; they cannot be sustained without this bread.

(L 13.15)

Through Your providence, Lord, provide the necessary means by which my soul may serve You at Your pleasure rather than at its own. Don't punish me by giving me what I want or desire if Your Love, which lives in me always, doesn't desire it. May this "I" die, and may another live in me greater than I and better for me than I, so that I may serve Him. May He live and give me life. May He reign, and may I be captive, for my soul doesn't want any other liberty.

(S 17.1–3)

I am aware in myself of neither happiness nor pain, however great. If certain things do give me either of these, the happiness or pain passes so quickly I marvel, and the feeling left me is that it was like a dream. This is the complete truth; for even though afterward I may want to rejoice over that happiness or be sad about that pain, it is not in my power to do so; just as a prudent person is unable to delight in or grieve over a dream he has had. The Lord has now awakened my soul from that which, because I was not mortified or dead to the things of the world, caused me such feelings; and His Majesty does not want my soul to become blind again.

(*L* 40.22)

So do not be tense, for if you begin to feel constrained, such a feeling will be very harmful to everything good, and at times you will end up being scrupulous and become incapable of doing anything for yourself or for others. And if you don't end up being scrupulous, this constraint will be good for you but it will not bring many souls to God because they will see so much repression and tenseness. Our nature is such that this constraint is frightening and oppressive to others, and they flee from following the road that you are taking, even though they know clearly that it is the more virtuous path. Another harm derives from this attitude; it is that of judging others.... If they have a holy joy, it will seem to be dissipation.... This constraint is detrimental to your neighbor. To think that if all do not proceed as you do, in this constrained way, they are not proceeding well is extremely wrong.

(*W* 41.5–6)

✤

The first effect is a forgetfulness of self, for truly the soul, seemingly, no longer is.... The soul doesn't worry about all that can happen. It experiences strange forgetfulness, for, as I say, seemingly the soul no longer is or would want to be anything in anything, except when it understands that there can come from itself something by which the glory and honor of God may increase even one degree. For this purpose the soul would very willingly lay down its life.

(*IC* 7.3.2)

The second effect is that the soul has a great desire to suffer, but not the kind of desire that disturbs it as previously. For the desire left in these souls that the will of God be done in them reaches such an extreme that they think everything His Majesty does is good. If He desires the soul to suffer, well and good; if not, it doesn't kill itself as it used to.

(IC 7.3.4)

These souls also have a deep interior joy when they are persecuted, with much more peace than that mentioned, and without any hostile feelings toward those who do, or desire to do, them evil. On the contrary, such a soul gains a particular love for its persecutors, in such a way that if it sees these latter in some trial it feels compassion and would take on any burden to free them from their trial, and eagerly recommends them to God and would rejoice to lose the favors His Majesty grants it if He would bestow these same gifts on those others so that they wouldn't offend our Lord.

(IC 7.3.5)

You have already seen the trials and afflictions these souls have experienced in order to die so as to enjoy our Lord. What surprises me most of all now is that they have just as great a desire to serve Him and that through them He be praised and that they may benefit some soul if they can. For not only do they not desire to die but they desire to live very many years suffering the greatest trials if through these they can help that the Lord be praised, even though in something very small. If they knew for certain that in leaving the body the soul would enjoy God, they wouldn't pay attention to that; nor do they think of the glory of the saints. They do not desire at that time to be in glory. Their glory lies in being able some way to help the Crucified, especially when they see He is so offended and that few there are who, detached from everything else, really look after His honor.

(IC 7.3.6)

There is a great detachment from everything and a desire to be always either alone or occupied in something that will benefit some soul. There are no interior trials or feelings of dryness, but the soul lives with a remembrance and tender love of our Lord. It would never want to go without praising Him. When it becomes distracted the Lord Himself awakens it.

(*IC* 7.3.8)

Every way in which the Lord helps the soul here, and all He teaches it, takes place with such quiet and so noiselessly.... In this His dwelling place, He alone and the soul rejoice together in the deepest silence. There is no reason for the intellect to stir or seek anything.... The faculties are not lost here; they do not work, but remain as though in amazement.

(*IC* 7.3.11)

I am amazed as well to see that when the soul arrives here all raptures are taken away. Only once in a while are they experienced and then without those transports and that flight of the spirit. They happen very rarely and almost never in public as they very often did before. Nor do the great occasions of devotion cause the soul concern as previously.... Now the reason could be that in this dwelling place either the soul has found its repose, or has seen so much that nothing frightens it, or that it doesn't feel that solitude it did before since it enjoys such company. In sum, Sisters, I don't know what the cause may be. For when the Lord begins to show what there is in this dwelling place and to bring the soul there, this great weakness is taken away. The weakness was a severe trial for the soul and previously was not taken away. Perhaps the reason is that the Lord has now fortified, enlarged, and made the soul capable.

(*IC* 7.3.12)

These effects, along with all the other good ones from the degrees of prayer we mentioned, are given by God when He brings the soul to Himself with this kiss sought by the bride, for I think this petition is here granted. Here an abundance of

water is given to this deer that was wounded. Here one delights in God's tabernacle. Here the dove Noah sent out to see
if the storm was over finds the olive branch as a sign of firm
ground discovered amid the floods and tempests of this world.
O Jesus! Who would know the many things there must be in
Scripture to explain this peace of soul! My God, since You see
how important it is for us, grant that Christians will seek it; and
in Your mercy do not take it away from those to whom You
have given it. For, in the end, people must always live with fear
until You give them true peace and bring them there where
that peace will be unending. I say "true peace," not because
this peace is not true but because the first war could return if
we were to withdraw from God....

The cross is not wanting but it doesn't disquiet or make
them lose peace. For the storms, like a wave, pass quickly. And
the fair weather returns, because the presence of the Lord they
experience makes them soon forget everything. May He be
ever blessed and praised by all His creatures, amen.

(*IC* 7.3.13–15)

You must not think, Sisters, that the effects I mentioned are always present in these souls. Hence, where I remember, I say
"ordinarily." For sometimes our Lord leaves these individuals in
their natural state, and then it seems all the poisonous creatures from the outskirts and other dwelling places of this castle
band together to take revenge for the time they were unable to
have these souls under their control.

True, this natural state lasts only a short while, a day at
most or a little more. And in this great disturbance, usually
occasioned by some event, the soul's gain through the good
company it is in becomes manifest. For the Lord gives the soul
great stability and good resolutions not to deviate from His service in anything. But it seems this determination increases, and
these souls do not deviate through even a very slight first movement. As I say this disturbance is rare, but our Lord does not
want the soul to forget its being, so that, for one thing, it might
always be humble; for another, that it might better understand

the tremendous favor it receives, what it owes His Majesty, and that it might praise Him.

(IC 7.4.1–2)

It will be good, Sisters, to tell you the reason the Lord grants so many favors in this world. Although, if you have paid attention, you will have understood this in learning of their effects, I want to tell you again here lest someone think that the reason is solely for the sake of giving delight to these souls; that thought would be a serious error. His Majesty couldn't grant us a greater favor than to give us a life that would be an imitation of the life His beloved Son lived. Thus I hold for certain that these favors are meant to fortify our weakness, as I have said here at times, that we may be able to imitate Him in His great sufferings.

We have always seen that those who were closest to Christ our Lord were those with the greatest trials. Let us look at what His glorious Mother suffered and the glorious apostles. How do you think St. Paul could have suffered such very great trials? Through him we can see the effects visions and contemplation produce when from our Lord, and not from the imagination or the devil's deceit. Did St. Paul by chance hide himself in the enjoyment of these delights and not engage in anything else? You already see that he didn't have a day of rest, from what we can understand, and neither did he have any rest at night since it was then that he earned his livelihood.

(IC 7.4.4–5)

How forgetful this soul, in which the Lord dwells in so particular a way, should be of its own rest, how little it should care for its honor, and how far it should be from wanting esteem in anything! For if it is with Him very much, as is right, it should think little about itself. All its concern is taken up with how to please Him more and how or where it will show Him the love it bears Him. This is the reason for prayer, my daughters, the purpose of this spiritual marriage: the birth always of good works, good works.

(IC 7.4.6)

This is the true sign of a thing, or favor, being from God, as I have already told you. It benefits me little to be alone making acts of devotion to our Lord, proposing and promising to do wonders in His service, if I then go away and when the occasion offers itself do everything the opposite.

(*IC* 7.4.7)

It seems to you that I am speaking with those who are beginning and that after this beginner's stage souls can rest. I have already told you that the calm these souls have interiorly is for the sake of their having much less calm exteriorly and much less desire to have exterior calm. . . . Being united with the Strong One through so sovereign a union of spirit with spirit, fortitude will cling to such a soul; and so we shall understand what fortitude the saints had for suffering and dying.

(*IC* 7.4.10)

This is what I want us to strive for, my Sisters; and let us desire and be occupied in prayer not for the sake of our enjoyment but so as to have this strength to serve. . . . Believe me, Martha and Mary must join together in order to show hospitality to the Lord and have Him always present and not host Him badly by failing to give Him something to eat. How would Mary, always seated at His feet, provide Him with food if her sister did not help her?

(*IC* 7.4.12)

Sometimes the devil gives us great desires so that we will avoid setting ourselves to the task at hand, serving our Lord in possible things, and instead be content with having desired the impossible. Apart from the fact that by prayer you will be helping greatly, you need not be desiring to benefit the whole world but must concentrate on those who are in your company, and thus your deed will be greater since you are more obliged toward them.

(*IC* 7.4.14)

❖

O charity of those who truly love this Lord and know their own nature! How little rest they can have if they see they may play a little part in getting even one soul to make progress and to love God more, or in consoling it, or in taking away some danger from it. How poorly would it then rest with this particular rest of its own!...I know personally some individuals...who brought me to understand this truth when I was greatly distressed to see myself with so little time. And I thus was sorry for them to see they were so occupied with so many business matters and things that obedience commanded them. I was thinking to myself, and even said so, that it wasn't possible in the midst of such commotion for the spirit to grow, for at that time they didn't have much spirit. O Lord, how different are your paths from our clumsy imaginings!...There was a person to whom I spoke a few days ago who for about fifteen years was kept so busy through obedience with work in occupations and government that in all those years he didn't remember having one day for himself, although he tried the best he could to keep a pure conscience and have some periods each day for prayer....He has found that he has, without knowing how, that same precious and desirable liberty of spirit that the perfect have. In it, they find all the happiness that could be wanted in this life, for in desiring nothing they possess all. Nothing on earth do they fear or desire, neither do trials disturb them, nor do consolations move them. In sum, nothing can take away their peace because these souls depend only on God. This is not the only person, for I have known others of the same sort, whom I had not seen for some, or many, years. I learned that the years were all spent in the fulfillment of the duties of obedience and charity. On the other hand, I saw such improvement in spiritual things that I was amazed. Well, come now, my daughters, don't be sad when obedience draws you to involvement in exterior matters. Know that if it is in the kitchen, the Lord walks among the pots and pans.

(*F* 5.5–8)

I met a religious who had resolved and become very deter-mined never to say "no" to anything his superior commanded no matter how much labor it would cost him. One day he was completely worn out from work; and when it was already late and he could no longer stay on his feet and went to sit down and rest a little, the superior met him and told him to take the hoe and go dig in the garden. He remained silent; although in his human nature he was indeed afflicted, for he couldn't help it. He took his hoe and when he was about to enter a passage-way into the garden (I saw the spot many years after he told me of this, for I managed to found a house in that place), our Lord appeared to him weighed down by the cross, so tired and worn that this religious understood clearly that what he himself was enduring was nothing when compared with what the Lord endured.

(*F* 5.9)

We must desire solitude even when involved in the things I'm speaking of; indeed, this desire is continually present in souls that truly love God.... [L]eaving solitude...makes us realize who we are and the degree of virtue we have. For people who are always recollected in solitude, however holy in their own opinion they may be, don't know whether they are patient or humble, nor do they have the means of knowing this. How could it be known whether a man were valiant if he were not seen in battle?...

It is a great good for us if we are ordered to do things that show us our own lowliness. I consider one day of hum-ble self-knowledge a greater favor from the Lord, even though the day may have cost us numerous afflictions and trials, than many days of prayer. Moreover, the true lover loves everywhere and is always thinking of the Beloved! It would be a thing hard to bear if we were able to pray only when off in some corner. I do realize that prayer in the midst of occupations can-not last many hours; but, O my Lord, what power over You a sigh of sorrow has that comes from the depths of our heart on seeing that it isn't enough that we are in this exile but that we are not even given the chance to be alone enjoying You....

Here we see clearly that we are His slaves, our wills being sold, out of love for Him, through the virtue of obedience since through obedience we in some way give up enjoying God Himself. And yet, this is nothing if we consider that He came from the bosom of His Father out of obedience to become our slave.... It is not the length of time spent in prayer that benefits one; when the time is spent as well in good works, it is a great help in preparing the soul for the enkindling of love. The soul may thereby be better prepared in a very short time than through many hours of reflection.

(F 5.15–17)

> In weeping be my joy,
> My rest in fright,
> In sorrowing my serenity,
> My wealth in losing all.
>
> Amid storms be my love,
> In the wound my delight.
> My life in death,
> In rejection my favor.
>
> In poverty be my riches,
> My triumph in struggling,
> Rest in laboring,
> In sadness my contentment.
>
> In darkness be my light,
> My greatness in the lowly place,
> My way on the short road,
> In the cross my glory.
>
> In humiliation be my honor,
> My palm in suffering
> Increase in my wanting
> In losing my gain.

My fullness be in hunger,
In fearing my hope,
My rejoicing in fear,
In grieving my delight.

In forgetting be my memory,
Humiliation my exalting,
In lowliness my repute,
Affronts my victory.

My laurels be in contempt,
In afflictions my fondness,
My dignity a lowly nook,
In solitude my esteem.

In Christ be my trust,
My affection in Him alone,
In His weariness my vigor,
My repose in His imitation.

My strength is founded here,
In Him alone my surety,
My integrity's proof,
In His likeness my purity.

(*P* 26)

Chronology

1515   Born in Avila on March 28.

1528   Doña Beatriz de Ahumada, Teresa's mother, dies.

1531   Enters the convent school of Our Lady of Grace.

1532   Returns home because of illness.

1535   November 2: enters Monastery of the Incarnation.

1538   Leaves the monastery for treatment in Becedas. Reads Osuna's *Third Spiritual Alphabet.*

1539   Seriously ill and returns to her father's home. Lapses into coma for four days. Brought back to the monastery; paralyzed for three years.

1542   Cured through the intercession of St. Joseph. Gives up prayer.

1543   Cares for her sick father; helps him in his death.

1544   Returns to prayer.

1554   During Lent, experiences a radical conversion before a statue of Christ at the pillar.

1556   In May receives the grace of spiritual betrothal.

1558   Friends say she is possessed.

1559   Intellectual visions of Christ begin.

1560   Beginning of the imaginative visions of the risen Christ, which Teresa is ordered to mock. Receives the grace of transverberation. St. Peter of Alcántara assures Teresa and others that her spiritual favors are from God. Discussions about a new foundation begin.

1562   January to June: resides in Toledo; meets García de Toledo, O.P.
Finishes first edition of the *Life* in June and returns from Toledo to Avila.
August 24: foundation of St. Joseph's.
Called back to the Monastery of the Incarnation.
December: Moves to St. Joseph's and changes name to Teresa de Jesús.

1563   Writes the *Constitutions* for St. Joseph's.

1565   July 17: Pius IV confirms the practice of poverty in the new monastery and its submission to the bishop.

1566   Teresa finishes *The Way of Perfection* and writes *Meditations on the Song of Songs*.

1567   Prior General Rubeo visits Avila and authorizes Teresa to found other monasteries.
August 15: foundation in Medina del Campo where Teresa meets St. John of the Cross.

1568   April: foundation in Malagón.
August 15: foundation in Valladolid where Teresa teaches St. John of the Cross her way of life.
November 28: first foundation of friars at Duruelo.

1569   May 14: foundation in Toledo.
June 23: foundation of nuns in Pastrana.
July 13: foundation of friars in Pastrana.
Writes *Soliloquies*.

1570   November 1: foundation in Salamanca.

1571   January 25: foundation in Alba de Tormes with St. John of the Cross.
October 14: Teresa installed as prioress of the Monastery of the Incarnation.

1572   St. John of the Cross becomes chaplain and confessor at the Incarnation monastery.
November 18: receives the grace of spiritual marriage.

1573   August 25: begins writing *Foundations.*

1574   March 19: foundation in Segovia with St. John of the Cross.
April 6–7: nuns abandon the foundation in Pastrana and move to Segovia.
Princess of Eboli denounces Teresa's *Life* to the Inquisition.

1575   February 24: foundation in Beas.
April–May: first meetings with Jerónimo Gracián.
May 24: vow of obedience to Gracián.
May 29: foundation in Seville.
August 12: Lorenzo returns from America.
December: denounced to Inquisition of Seville.
Struggles with the Calced. Receives orders from chapter at Piacenza to retire to one of her convents in Castile.

1576   January 1: foundation in Caravaca by Ana de San Alberto, at Teresa's orders.
June 23: arrives in Toledo.
August: writes *On Making the Visitation.* Continues *Foundations.*
Persecution intensifies.

1577   June 2: begins to write *The Interior Castle.*
July: arrives in Avila.

November 29: finishes *The Interior Castle.*
December 3: St. John of the Cross taken prisoner.
December 24: Teresa falls down the stairs at St. Joseph's
and breaks her left arm.

1578   August 17–18: St. John of the Cross escapes from his
prison in Toledo.
October 16: Teresian friars and nuns placed under the
authority of the Calced.
The most troubled year for the Reform.

1579   End of persecutions.
June: begins traveling again.
November 24: arrives in Malagón and hastens work on
the new convent.

1580   February: foundation in Villanueva de la Jara.
March: travels to Toledo and becomes seriously ill.
June 22: papal brief allows Teresian friars and nuns to
form a separate province.
June 26: Lorenzo dies.
August 8: seriously ill in Valladolid.
December 28: foundation in Palencia.

1581   Chapter at Alcalá; *Constitutions* confirmed and printed.
March 4: Gracián elected provincial.
June 30: foundation in Soria.

1582   January 2: leaves Avila for the last time to begin foun-
dation in Burgos.
January 20: foundation in Granada made by St. John of
the Cross and Ana de Jesús.
April 19: foundation in Burgos completed.
September 20: reaches Alba de Tormes.
September 29: goes to bed seriously ill, never to get up
again; announces her death.
October 3: receives the Sacrament of Extreme Unction
and makes her last confession.

October 4: dies at the age of sixty-seven. (The Gregorian calendar was introduced that year; the day following Teresa's death became October 15.)

1614   April 24: beatified by Paul V.

1622   March 12: canonized by Gregory XV with Saints Isidore, Ignatius Loyola, Francis Xavier, and Philip Neri.

1970   September 27: declared the first woman doctor of the church by Paul VI.